THE SEA OF JAPAN

JAPAN LIBRARY

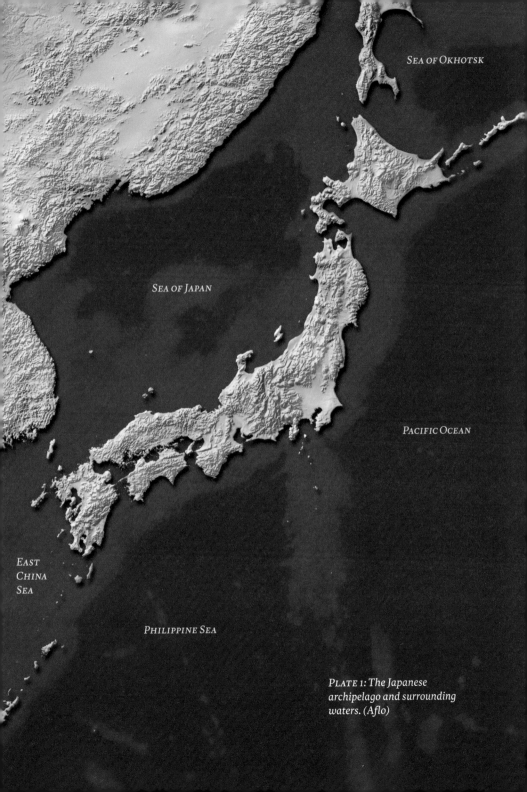

SEA OF OKHOTSK

SEA OF JAPAN

PACIFIC OCEAN

EAST
CHINA
SEA

PHILIPPINE SEA

PLATE 1: *The Japanese archipelago and surrounding waters. (Aflo)*

PLATE 2: *Primeval beech forests in the Shirakami Mountains nourished by abundant precipitation from the Sea of Japan (Photo by Masami Goto/Aflo). (Figure 5-2)*

PLATE 3: *The* funaya *(boathouses) of Ine are uniquely suited to the weak tides experienced in bays along the Sea of Japan coast. (Figure 1-3)*

PLATE 4: *The first-generation research vessel (R/V)* Hakuho Maru *(displacement: 3226 t; operated by the University of Tokyo) was built in 1967 and operated until 1988. Currently, the second-generation* Hakuho Maru *(displacement: 3991 t) is operated by the Japan Agency for Marine-Earth Science and Technology (JAMSTEC) (see column at the end of chapter 6 for details). (Figure 3-7)*

PLATE 5: *Map of countries in East Asia and the Sea of Japan region. Reproduced with permission from Toyama Prefecture. (Figure 6-11)*

環 日 本 海 ・ 東 ア ジ ア 諸 国 図

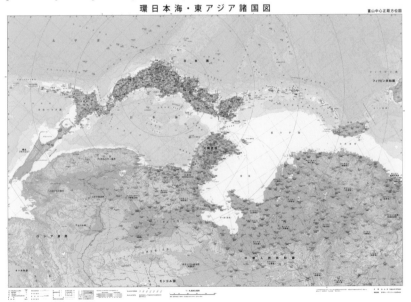

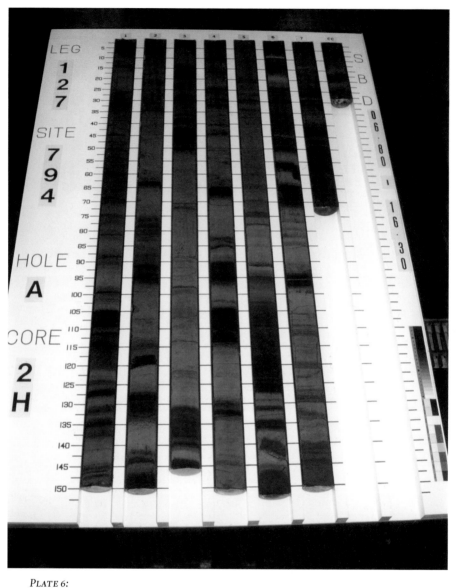

PLATE 6:
Halved sediment core collected from the Sea of Japan in 1989 by the Ocean Drilling Program (photograph courtesy of Ryuji Tada). (Figure 4-5)

THE SEA OF JAPAN

GAMO Toshitaka

Translated by Gen Del Raye

Unraveling the
Mystery of Its
Hidden Depths

Note: The modified Hepburn system of romanization (as found in Kenkyusha's New Japanese-English Dictionary) is utilized for Japanese words, but macrons are not used except for citations and references to works that were published with macrons. All names are given with given name preceding surname.

The Sea of Japan: Unraveling the Mystery of Its Hidden Depths
Toshitaka Gamo. Translated by Gen Del Raye.

Published by
Japan Publishing Industry Foundation for Culture (JPIC)
2-2-30 Kanda-Jinbocho, Chiyoda-ku, Tokyo 101-0051, Japan

First English edition: March 2021

This book is a translation of *Nihonkai: Sono shinso de okotteiru koto* (Kodansha, Ltd., 2016).
English publishing rights arranged with Kodansha, Ltd., Tokyo.

Book design: Andrew Pothecary (itsumo music)

Printed in Japan
ISBN 978-4-86658-129-3
https://japanlibrary.jpic.or.jp/

Contents

Introduction to the English Edition

Toshitaka Gamo

Welcome to the Sea of Japan!

In recent years, more and more scientists have turned their attention to the waters around the Japanese archipelago. Some of these scientists are oceanographers, of course, but others include experts in the fields of fisheries science, marine mineral and energy resources, and global environmental science. Their interest has focused especially on a body of water cut off from the broader Pacific by the arc of the Japanese archipelago, or in other words, the Sea of Japan.

What could be so special about the Sea of Japan? I set out to answer this question in detail in this book. I specialize in chemical oceanography (the study of ocean chemistry), and in the course of my research, I have participated in numerous research cruises in the Sea of Japan. In writing this book, I sought to examine the characteristics of the Sea of Japan from many angles. In doing so, I was constantly reminded of and amazed by the myriad phenomena and mysteries contained within this small sea, as well as by its fundamental importance to Japanese history.

By exploring these mysteries in a clear and organized way, I hoped that the book would help renew the Japanese public's interest in and appreciation of the Sea of Japan. As such, I was delighted that Kodansha Bluebacks agreed to publish it in 2016. It goes without saying, however, that the Sea of Japan's importance stretches far beyond Japan. In fact, I increasingly began to feel that it was important for people around the world to learn about the Sea of Japan. Just as I was thinking about what to do, I received the wonderful news of the forthcoming publication of an English edition of my book.

While re-reading the text in the process of preparing for the publication of the English edition, I realized that the book contained many passages that would have been self-explanatory to Japanese readers but quite baffling to English-speaking ones. Although the content of the book remains largely unchanged, some passages have been rewritten for clarity, and new figures and explanatory text were added where needed. I think the result is a book that even readers who are unfamiliar with Japan will find both fascinating and easy to understand.

Since antiquity, the maritime people of Japan have benefited enormously from the oceans, and have cherished and sought to coexist with the ocean environment. In interacting with other countries that border the Sea of Japan, they have also shaped a history that includes both shared prosperity and terrible conflict. In the past, as today, the people of the region have often sought peace across the ocean and cherished and tried to learn from the sea. My greatest hope is that many of you who read this book will come to feel familiar with the "miniature ocean" of the Sea of Japan and understand the importance of conserving it for the future.

I am grateful to the following people for their help with the English translation: Kiyoshi Nakaizumi, Futsuki Asonuma, Hiroshi Makino, and Haruna Sawada at the Japan Publishing Industry Foundation for Culture; Rick Weisburd, Gen Del Raye, Shinichiro Egawa, David Jones, and Mika Kido at ELSS, Inc.; and Marica Nishitani at Kodansha. I thank Kyoko Okino at the Atmosphere and Ocean Research Institute, the University of Tokyo, for providing the bathymetric map of the Sea of Japan. I am especially indebted to Takashi Kurata at Kodansha Bluebacks for his tireless support and encouragement not just during the translation process, but also throughout the process of writing the Japanese edition.

Prologue

The Japanese archipelago and the Sea of Japan to its northwest are profoundly and inextricably linked.

This linkage is explored as an epic disaster story in *Nippon Chinbotsu* (Japan Sinks), a 1973 science fiction novel by Sakyo Komatsu that depicts a scenario in which an anomaly in the crust and mantle causes the Japanese archipelago to sink into the ocean. It sold around 4 million copies to become a record-breaking best-seller and became the basis for feature-length films in 1973 and 2006. Some of you may also be familiar with TV or radio adaptations.

It goes without saying that *Japan Sinks* is a work of fiction; but for a moment, let's consider the scenario it depicts. How would it affect the Sea of Japan? First of all, the Japanese archipelago, which separates the Sea of Japan from the Pacific Ocean, would disappear. This would mean that the Sea of Japan would become part of the Pacific, and the name "Sea of Japan" itself would become obsolete.

Or let's consider the opposite scenario. What if the Sea of Japan disappeared? In fact, the Japanese archipelago was once part of the Eurasian continent. The Sea of Japan was only created once the Japanese archipelago broke off from the continent about 15–20 million years ago. If the Sea of Japan disappeared, the Japanese archipelago would once again become part of the Eurasian continent. In this scenario, the term "Japanese archipelago" would become essentially meaningless.

I suspect that many people think of the Sea of Japan, when they think of it at all, in the same way we think of the air we breathe. That is, we tend to take its presence for granted. This is a mistake. In fact, the Sea of Japan is an indispensable asset that provides countless benefits to the Japanese archipelago. In this book, I will describe the surprising hidden functions performed by the Sea of Japan and discuss its importance from various perspectives. I hope you'll stick with me until the end of my story.

But first, let me introduce myself. I am (I think) an ordinary ocean-ographer, not particularly good with people, and with an optimistic personality. I work at the Atmosphere and Ocean Research Institute on the University of Tokyo's Kashiwa Campus. After graduating from the Department of Chemistry in the School of Science at the same university more than 40 years ago, I joined this research institute as a graduate student (at the time, it was called the "Ocean Research Institute" and was located on the Nakano Campus), which means I have spent the majority of my life at the institute. I have spent this time being fasci-nated by the oceans, which cover some 70% of the Earth's surface and yet are full of mysteries, and have whiled away many days observing and studying the chemistry of the oceans from various perspectives.

Seawater physics and chemistry, which include properties like tem-perature and salinity, are fundamental characteristics of the oceans. Although it is well known that the main dissolved component of sea-water is sodium chloride (i.e., table salt), the full list of components includes a host of other chemicals. For example, there are metallic ele-ments such as calcium, magnesium, iron, zinc, and copper; radioactive elements such as uranium and plutonium; and dissolved gasses such as oxygen and carbon dioxide. . . . The list goes on.

Each of these components provides an oceanographer with innu-merable potential research questions, which include each component's precise concentrations and concentration distributions and any gradi-ents across time and space, as well as the ways in which the components may interact with various processes such as ocean circulation, biological activity, marine pollution, seafloor hydrothermal activity, and global climate change. Each of these questions is important for understanding the environment of the planet on which we live. The foremost method of addressing these questions is to actually conduct measurements in the ocean; in other words, to step aboard a research ship and collect water samples. Then, carry out precise chemical analyses in shipboard or land-based laboratories to gradually accumulate an informative dataset.

In addition to studying the vast open spaces of the Pacific and Indian

Oceans, I have had many opportunities to investigate the waters around Japan. So far, I have participated in a total of eight research cruises in the Sea of Japan. The first of these was in 1977, meaning that I have been doing this for over 40 years. At the time, I was a doctoral student whose research projects had only just started to gather steam. Because the Sea of Japan borders the Japanese island of Honshu, it is comparatively easy to access; it has the closeness and familiarity of a backyard that you can step into just by opening a door in your house. Other than in the winter, the waves are generally calm; this keeps the research ship stable and facilitates sample collection and other observations.

In my first research cruise in the Sea of Japan, we collected huge amounts of seawater from depths of over 3000 m. Later, once I had returned to shore, I used these samples to make the first ever measurements of carbon-14 (a radionuclide) in the deep water of the Sea of Japan. Using these data, I became the first person to determine the time scale of the Sea of Japan's deep-water circulation, which became the focus of my doctoral thesis.

In some ways, it is understandable that the Sea of Japan is often overlooked. By area, it accounts for only 0.3% of the area of the global oceans. In this respect, it is truly a miniature ocean. Yet in terms of the processes at work, the Sea of Japan actually contains many of the dynamics that you would expect of the biggest oceans.

More than 20 years ago, I published an article about the Sea of Japan in the monthly magazine *Kagaku* (Science) published by Iwanami Shoten. In it, I wrote that "deep water circulation in the Sea of Japan is so extensive that you could consider it a miniature version of the global ocean circulation system." To be honest, at the time I was worried that this statement might have gone a little too far.

Luckily, it has subsequently been corroborated by some 20 years' worth of data collected by researchers from Japan and elsewhere, and the phrase "miniature ocean" has since caught on among the public as a nickname for the Sea of Japan. In fact, research has shown that the Sea of Japan is not only a miniature version of the global oceans but is also a harbinger of future global environmental change. Like a canary in a coal mine, impending changes in the wider oceans seem to become visible much earlier in the Sea of Japan. For this reason, the Sea of Japan has attracted attention from researchers around the world.

Of course, the Sea of Japan can help us understand the past as well. A unique culture evolved among the early residents of the Japanese archipelago thanks to the many benefits provided by the Sea of Japan.

It is often said that the Earth is located within a "habitable (or Goldilocks) zone" of optimum distance from the sun, meaning that it is neither too far from nor too close to the sun's warmth. The Japanese archipelago has a similar relationship to the Eurasian continent. It is neither too close nor too far. In other words, the Sea of Japan is just the right size. If the Sea of Japan were bigger or smaller than it is now, the environment of the Japanese archipelago and the history of the people living there would have turned out completely differently. It is not an exaggeration to say that a "different Japan" would have developed in this alternate reality.

The Sea of Japan has had a profound and fundamental influence on the Japanese archipelago and on Japanese lives. At the same time, it is a "miniature ocean" that is the focus of worldwide attention. What mysteries might be hidden in this most familiar of seas? Without any further ado, let's set sail for this fascinating ocean.

What Are the Features of the Sea of Japan?

The Sea of Japan, which is bounded by the Eurasian continent and the Japanese archipelago, is one of several "marginal seas" that are found in the western Pacific Ocean. Although it is almost completely enclosed by land masses, the maximum depth of the Sea of Japan (about 3800 m) is similar to the average depth of the open ocean; also, it contains an independent internal circulation, which sets it apart from neighboring seas.

In winter, cold and dry northwesterly monsoon winds blow in from Siberia and trigger a process that circulates the deep waters of the Sea of Japan. At the same time, the monsoon winds absorb large amounts of moisture from the sea surface and deposit it as snow on the Japanese archipelago. This process is crucial in maintaining Japan's humid climate and lush natural environment.

Wak
Hokkaido
Honshu
Sea of Japan
JAPAN
Osaka Yokohama
Shimonoseki
Tokyo

1-1
The Sea of Japan is a "Deep Bathtub" in the Western North Pacific

The Sea of Japan is an example of a marginal sea, which is a relatively enclosed body of seawater that exists on the outer edge of a continent and is separated from the open ocean by islands or peninsulas.

The western margin of the North Pacific contains a string of many similarly-sized marginal seas, as seen in figure 1-1: from north to south, the Sea of Okhotsk, the Sea of Japan, the Yellow Sea, the East China Sea, the South China Sea, the Sulu Sea, and the Celebes Sea. For the purposes of this discussion, we can say that each marginal sea is akin to a bathtub (for the moment, we will say that the much larger Pacific Ocean is, for example, an Olympic swimming pool). Some of these "bathtubs" are shallow, and others are quite deep. What about this book's protagonist, the Sea of Japan? The Sea of Japan has an average depth of 1667 m and

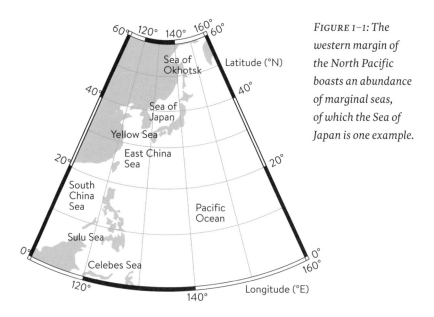

FIGURE 1-1: The western margin of the North Pacific boasts an abundance of marginal seas, of which the Sea of Japan is one example.

a maximum depth of 3796 m. These depths are less than half the corresponding depths for the oceans overall (average depth: 3729 m; maximum depth: 10,920 m in the Mariana Trench), but when the average depth of the Sea of Japan is compared against those of other nearby marginal seas (e.g., Yellow Sea and East China Sea: 272 m; Sea of Okhotsk: 973 m), we can see that the Sea of Japan is by far the deepest (all depths are as listed in *Rikanenpyo* [Chronological Scientific Tables]). In fact, the Sea of Japan's maximum depth (3796 m) is enough to completely submerge Japan's highest mountain, Mount Fuji (elevation 3776 m).

The surface area of the Sea of Japan is 1.0×10^6 km^2. This is only about 0.3% of the total surface area of the oceans (362×10^6 km^2). In addition, the volume of the Sea of Japan is 1.7×10^6 km^3, which is 0.13% of the total volume of the oceans (1350×10^6 km^3). In comparison with the world's oceans as a whole, the Sea of Japan is truly just a small part.

≋

1–2
What Does the Bottom of the Bathtub Look Like?
The Bathymetry of the Sea of Japan

What does the bottom of the Sea of Japan look like? Figure 1-2 is a map of the bathymetry (depths) of the region. The first thing you may notice is that the Sea of Japan has a hill in its center. This hill is called the "Yamato Rise": it was named after the survey vessel *Yamato*, owned by the Japanese Navy, which was used to discover the rise in 1924. (Although this vessel shares its name with the battleship *Yamato*, which famously sank in a battle near the end of World War II, it is, of course, a different ship.)

The terms "rise" and "ridge" in the context of the seafloor refer to elongated underwater hills (i.e., seamounts or banks) with largely flat summits. Such areas are favorable habitats for fish and shellfish and often support productive fishing grounds. The summit of the Yamato Rise is just 236 m below sea level.

You might also notice the presence in the map of three "basins"

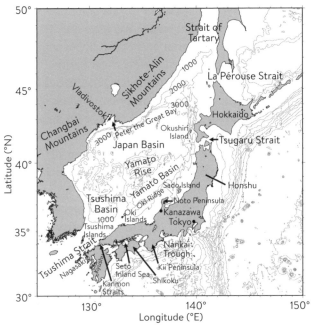

FIGURE 1–2: *Map of the bathymetry of the Sea of Japan showing the four main straits that connect it to surrounding seas and oceans. The bathymetry data are according to ETOPO1 (https://www.ngdc.noaa.gov/mgg/global/). The names of undersea features are as listed in the General Bathymetric Chart of the Ocean Gazetteer version 3.0+204 (https://www.gebco.net/). The depth contours are every 1000 meters.*

(depressions in the seafloor) arranged around the Yamato Rise. These are the Japan Basin, a large basin located to the north of the Yamato Rise, which occupies almost the entire northern half of the Sea of Japan; the Yamato Basin, located to the southeast of the Rise; and the Tsushima Basin, located to the southwest of the Rise.

The Japan Basin is the deepest of the three, with a maximum depth of approximately 3800 m, followed by the Yamato Basin (approximately 3000 m), and finally by the Tsushima Basin (approximately 2600 m). These depths were estimated from marine charts or from bathymetry data collected during ship-based surveys.

South of the Yamato Rise is a mound named the Oki Ridge. The Oki Islands are located near the southwest end of this ridge.

The Yamato Rise and its southern extension form a continuous shape that stretches northward from the Japanese archipelago in an arrangement that roughly resembles the shape of a bent spoon. Although this is purely a coincidence, it's interesting to note that this "bent spoon" shape is a larger version of the shape of the Noto Peninsula, which also extends into the Sea of Japan. Thanks to the Oki Ridge and Yamato Rise, the Sea of Japan has a rugged bottom instead of the flat and smooth bottom you might expect from your bathtub at home.

Finally, the map shows four straits—from north to south, the Strait of Tartary (also known as the Mamiya Strait), the La Pérouse Strait (also known as the Soya Strait), the Tsugaru Strait, and the Tsushima Strait (also known as the Korea Strait)—that connect the Sea of Japan to surrounding seas and oceans. (Strictly speaking, the Kanmon Straits also lead out of the Sea of Japan, but because they are much smaller than the other four straits, I will omit them from the following discussion.)

≋

1–3
Why Does the Sea of Japan Have Weak Tides?

Here, I will focus on the shallowness of the four straits. A strait is in effect a "threshold" that separates two adjacent oceans or seas, where the shallowness of the strait corresponds to the height of the threshold. You might say, for example, that a certain institution or business has a "high threshold" for entry. Similarly, the shallower a strait, the more difficult it is for deep water to pass through.

The depths of the Strait of Tartary, and the La Pérouse, Tsugaru, and Tsushima Straits are roughly 10, 50, 130, and 130 m, respectively. Compare this against the average depth of the Sea of Japan (1667 m) and you can see that the straits are indeed very shallow (i.e., the thresholds are high).

FIGURE 1-3: *The* funaya *(boathouses) of Ine are uniquely suited to the weak tides experienced in bays along the Sea of Japan coast.*

In other words, although the bathtub known as the Sea of Japan has four channels (i.e., straits) leading to adjacent seas or oceans, each of these channels is extremely narrow and shallow. The narrowness and shallowness of the straits strongly hinders exchange of deep water through them: this bathymetric isolation is the first important characteristic of the Sea of Japan. As I will explore later in detail, this is not simply a matter of bathymetry but is also intimately related to internal circulation patterns and seawater composition in the Sea of Japan.

One relatively familiar example of the consequences of the arrangement of the straits is that the tidal range (the extent of the rising and falling of the tides) is much smaller in the Sea of Japan than on the Pacific side of the Japanese archipelago. To cite one case that happened to catch my eye, during a recent spring tide in Aomori Prefecture (fig. 1-3), the tidal range in Hachinohe, which is on the Pacific coast, was 130 cm, while that in nearby Fukaura, which faces the Sea of Japan, was only 20 cm.

This difference is caused by the highly enclosed nature of the Sea of Japan, or in other words, by the narrowness and shallowness of the straits. During high or low tides, when the water level in the Sea of Japan either rises or falls, seawater must either flow in or out from the surrounding oceans. However, because all four straits into and out of the Sea of Japan are shallow and narrow, large volumes of seawater cannot pass through them in a short time. This is why the tidal range in the Sea of Japan is so small.

This small tidal range poses a problem if you are looking to dig for clams in exposed tidal flats, but it does have the benefit of enabling the construction of houses right up to the limit of the coastline. For example, the *funaya* (boathouses) of Ine, located in the western part of Wakasa Bay in Kyoto Prefecture, are part of what are known as "floating villages" and have become popular tourist destinations (fig. 1-3, plate 3).

≋

1–4
Why Is the Sea of Japan So Rich in Fishery Resources? The Confluence of Warm and Cold Currents

Presently, only one current flows into the Sea of Japan from the open ocean. As shown in figure 1-4, this is the Tsushima Warm Current, which flows through the Tsushima Strait.

The existence of the Tsushima Warm Current is the second important characteristic of the Sea of Japan. The effects of this current will be a recurring theme in various chapters of this book.

When we examine the origin of the Tsushima Warm Current, we find that it involves two separate ocean currents. The first of these, a subbranch of the warm Kuroshio Current, is thought to diverge from the main branch in the waters south of the island of Kyushu. The other is the Taiwan Warm Current, which flows northward from the vicinity of the Taiwan Strait and incorporates terrestrial runoff from the Yangtze River on its way to the Sea of Japan.

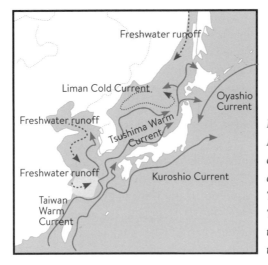

FIGURE 1–4:
A map of ocean currents around the Japanese archipelago (adapted from Tomoharu Senju). The Tsushima Warm Current is the only current flowing into the Sea of Japan.

These two currents converge near the Tsushima Strait (the mixing ratio of the two currents is thought to differ across seasons) and flow into the Sea of Japan. Compared to the main branch of the Kuroshio Current that flows past the southern coast of Honshu Island, the Tsushima Warm Current has about one-tenth the flow volume and one-quarter the flow speed.

This Tsushima Warm Current is responsible for the warm and humid climate of the Japanese archipelago along the Sea of Japan. Also, by transporting the relatively saline water of the Kuroshio Current into the surface waters of the Sea of Japan, the Tsushima Warm Current plays a role in generating the high-density surface water needed to drive vertical mixing (I will explain this in detail later in the chapter).

The Tsushima Warm Current takes about two months to traverse the Sea of Japan, during which time it forms multiple branches and eddies, before flowing into the Pacific Ocean through the Tsugaru and La Pérouse Straits.

Additionally, part of the Tsushima Warm Current flows to the northern-most reaches of the Sea of Japan, namely the Strait of Tartary, where the water becomes colder. The input of cold fresh water from the Amur River cools the water mass even further before it flows southward along the northwestern margin of the Sea of Japan (i.e., the Eurasian coastline). This current is known as the Liman Cold Current (see fig. 1-4). The boundary between the Tsushima Warm Current and the Liman Cold Current, which flow in opposite directions, is characterized by rapid changes in temperature and salinity. This is known as a "subpolar front," and is a productive fishing ground where many fishes (e.g., Japanese pilchard, chub mackerel, Japanese horse mackerel, yellowtail, and Japanese sandfish) that migrate northward with the Tsushima Warm Current take advantage of the abundant food stocks of the Liman Cold Current and breed.

The topography of the Yamato Rise deflects ocean currents upward, bringing nutrient-rich intermediate and deep water to the surface, which in turn boosts plankton stocks and provides more food for fish populations. This process plays a major role in supporting the Sea of Japan's productive fisheries.

≋

1–5
Functions of the Winter Monsoon

Japan is blessed with a variety of seasons that each have their own charm and beauty on both land and sea. In the Sea of Japan, however, winter is surely the most iconic season.

In winter, the Japanese coastline along the Sea of Japan is often subjected to cold northwesterly monsoon winds originating from an air mass known as the Siberian High, which produces severely cold weather. The Sea of Japan absorbs the kinetic energy of these monsoon winds and unleashes roaring swells that crash onto the shore. In ancient times, the storm-tossed surface of the Sea of Japan in winter may have inspired fear and been the cause of many sleepless nights among those who had to listen to the bellowing waves.

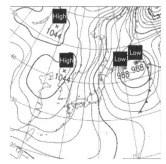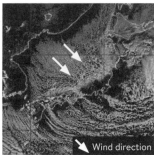

FIGURE 1–5: A pressure map (left panel) and satellite image (right panel) showing the atmospheric pressure pattern known as "western high, eastern low." This pressure pattern is emblematic of wintertime conditions in Japan.

The atmospheric pressure pattern known as "western high, eastern low" is familiar to anyone who follows Japanese wintertime weather forecasts. The northwesterly monsoon winds that drive the creation of this severe winter weather pattern are the third key characteristic of the Sea of Japan.

Northwesterly monsoon winds have two main effects on the Sea of Japan: First, they bring large snowfall totals to the Japanese archipelago. Second, they have a strong cooling effect on surface waters, which in turn drives vertical mixing in the Sea of Japan. The Tsushima Warm Current also plays an important supporting role in both of these effects.

1-5-1 THE SEA OF JAPAN IS A NATURAL DESALINATION DEVICE

Let's start by examining the first effect. When cold and dry monsoon winds blow strongly from the Eurasian continent onto the Sea of Japan, they encounter water that has been warmed by the Tsushima Warm Current. This combination is a recipe for rapid evaporation from the sea surface. The newly generated water vapor rises into the atmosphere, where it cools, condenses, and forms snow-bearing clouds.

Massed lines of snow-bearing clouds filling the sky over the Sea of

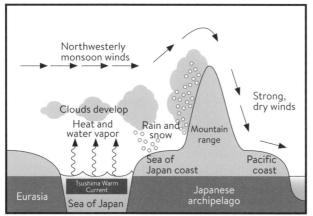

Japan are a quintessential sight during the Japanese winter. Satellite images of such clouds are often shown during TV weather forecasts to indicate the development of a western high, eastern low pressure pattern (fig. 1-5).

Winter monsoon winds blow snow-bearing clouds across the Sea of Japan, where they collide with the mountain ranges that make up the spine of the Japanese archipelago (e.g., the Ou Mountains, the Japan Alps, and the Chugoku Mountains). As the clouds rise over these mountains, they cool and deposit massive amounts of snow on plains and mountains along the Sea of Japan coast. Having deposited their moisture in the form of snow, the now dry and cold monsoon winds descend onto the Pacific side of the archipelago in the form of strong downdrafts (fig. 1-6).

At times, areas that experience extreme blizzards and heavy snowfalls (i.e., the "Special Heavy-Snowfall Areas") are subjected to road closures and the cutting off of villages from outside help, which can impose substantial social and economic costs. On the other hand, winter snowfall events are essential to maintaining Japan's abundant water reserves and internationally renowned ski resorts.

Of course, even though the snow that falls over Japan is crystallized fresh water, it originates in the saltwater of the Sea of Japan. And whereas ocean water is not suitable for drinking, fresh water is. In other words, the Sea of Japan in winter acts as a vast desalination device. A desalination device is a piece of equipment that is used in arid regions and aboard ocean-going vessels, among other applications, to convert seawater to fresh water. The Sea of Japan is a natural desalination device that creates fresh water from the large-scale evaporation of seawater, and then delivers this water to the Japanese archipelago.

Snow that falls in mountainous regions does not melt quickly. Although some portion of it will gradually melt into rivers and flow back into the oceans, another portion seeps into the soil and contributes to long-term groundwater storage.

Some of the bottled water that we unthinkingly drink may also have once existed as seawater in the Sea of Japan. Fresh water is necessary for sustaining life in humans and nearly all other land creatures. In regions that suffer from water scarcity, some countries are forced to invest huge quantities of energy into creating fresh water from seawater. By contrast, the Sea of Japan delivers abundant fresh water to Japan completely free of charge. Residents of the Japanese archipelago have, since its initial settlement, reaped untold benefits from this natural desalination device. Even today, it is in no way an overstatement to say that the Sea of Japan is a central pillar of Japan's water supply.

1-5-2 WATER CIRCULATION IN THE SEA OF JAPAN

The second important function of the northwesterly monsoon winds is that they cool the surface waters of the Sea of Japan and increase evaporation, thereby increasing its density (i.e., making it heavier). This effect is especially pronounced in the northern and northwestern reaches of the Sea of Japan, along the coastline of the Eurasian continent.

Unlike fresh water, which reaches maximum density at a temperature of 4°C, seawater becomes more and more dense (i.e., it becomes heavier) as it cools all the way to its freezing point (around –1.8°C). Also, seawater becomes heavier with increasing salinity. Previously, I explained that the Tsushima Warm Current supplies relatively high-salinity water to the Sea of Japan (see section 1-4).

When a parcel of seawater is cooled to its freezing point and parts of it begin to freeze, the remaining liquid water becomes saltier. This is because frozen sea ice does not contain salt, meaning that while freezing, the salt that is contained in the freezing seawater is expelled into the surrounding seawater.

Seawater that has increased in density (i.e., become heavier) sinks due to the action of gravity. Given sufficient density, this water may sink several thousand meters to the bottom of the ocean. The sinking water is replaced in equal measure by deep water that upwells toward the surface. This is the same principle that operates when you push a bucket down into the water of a bath: the bucket pushes surface water downward and causes the deeper water in the bath to rise by an equivalent amount.

The result of all of this is that the surface water mixes with deep water, or in other words, the Sea of Japan becomes vertically mixed. When the sinking of cold, salty, high-density surface water drives seawater circulation in this way, it is known as "thermohaline circulation," where "thermo" refers to heat (or temperature) and "haline" refers to salt (or salinity).

The stronger and colder the winter monsoon winds become, the more likely they are to generate high-density surface water, which drives increased sinking (i.e., downwelling). This sinking seawater sets off a chain of events, whereby the displacement of deeper water causes some of it to upwell to the surface. Figure 1-7 shows a schematic representation of this mode of seawater transport.

Conditions for the formation of dense surface water are particularly favorable in winter along the northern and northwestern coastline of the Sea of Japan. The Peter the Great Bay and its offshore waters off the coast of Vladivostok (the administrative center of Primorsky Krai, Russia) are especially active regions for surface-water downwelling. The main reason for this is the topography of the surrounding landmass.

Vladivostok is located between the Sikhote-Alin Mountain Range in Primorsky Krai and the Changbai Mountains at the northern edge of the

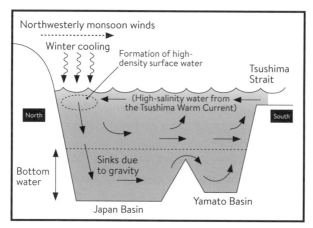

FIGURE 1–7: Schematic diagram of thermohaline circulation in the Sea of Japan.

Korean Peninsula (see fig. 1-2). These two mountain ranges funnel north-westerly monsoon winds into the gap between them (i.e., Vladivostok and its vicinity), and the strong cooling effect of this intense wind causes an especially strong decline in surface water temperature offshore of Vladivostok. As I will discuss in detail in chapter 6, in this area, oceano-graphic surveys directly observed the downwelling of surface water to the ocean bottom during the winter of 2000–2001.

≈

1–6
Three Major Characteristics of the Sea of Japan

As we have seen throughout this chapter, despite our tendency to take the Sea of Japan for granted, it is in fact a unique marginal sea with numerous unusual characteristics. These characteristics will feature throughout the rest of this book, so let's take a moment now to review them.

Here are three important characteristics of the Sea of Japan:

1. It is topographically isolated from other seas and oceans, and the straits that lead out of it are narrow and shallow.

2. It continually receives input from the Tsushima Warm Current.

3. It is exposed to northwesterly monsoon winds in winter.

In this chapter, I introduced the concepts that will be covered in this book by comparing the bathymetric features of the Sea of Japan, a marginal sea in the western North Pacific, to a "deep bathtub."

This "bathtub" has a maximum depth of 3800 m, and is only connected to surrounding seas and oceans by four straits. Because all of the straits are narrow and shallow, there is limited interchange with nearby seas and oceans. Even the deepest straits (the Tsushima and Tsugaru Straits) are only 130 m deep. Seawater contained in surface layers up to this depth can pass through the straits into or out of the Sea of Japan, but deeper water layers cannot.

The Tsushima Warm Current, which is the product of the merging of one branch of the Kuroshio Current with the Taiwan Warm Current, is the only surface current that flows into the Sea of Japan. This current helps maintain the Sea of Japan's elevated surface salinity, and also creates the mild climate of the Japanese archipelago along the Sea of Japan coast.

In winter, the Sea of Japan is exposed to severely cold northwesterly monsoon winds. These monsoon winds have two main impacts on the region that heavily influence conditions on the Japanese archipelago and in the Sea of Japan.

First, they absorb water vapor from the surface of the Sea of Japan to create massive snow-bearing clouds that deposit large amounts of snow (i.e., fresh water) on the Japanese archipelago. Second, they lower the temperature and raise the salinity of surface waters in the northern and northwestern reaches of the Sea of Japan, thereby increasing the density, which causes surface-water downwelling and promotes vertical mixing through a mechanism known as "thermohaline circulation."

This phenomenon of thermohaline circulation is by no means unique to the Sea of Japan. In fact, the same mechanism is responsible for large-scale water circulation in other oceans around the world. In chapter 2, I will begin by discussing this similarity to try to understand why the Sea of Japan is attracting attention around the world as a "miniature version of the global oceans."

~~~~~~~~~~~~~~~~~~~~~ *Column 1* ~~~~~~~~~~~~~~~~~~~~~

The Black Sea: Another "Bathtub"

The Black Sea is an inland sea on Asia's western border. It is surrounded by six countries: Turkey, Bulgaria, Romania, Ukraine, Russia, and Georgia. In surface area, it is about half the size of the Sea of Japan, and it has a maximum depth of 2250 m. This is not quite as deep of the Sea of Japan, but it is still comparable to the depth of the open ocean.

The Black Sea is also highly enclosed, and as with the Sea of Japan, it is a bathtub-like basin. Although it is connected to the Mediterranean through the Sea of Marmara, the two straits (the Bosporus and Dardanelles) that link these seas are very shallow (maximum depths of 35 and 65 m, respectively), and all deeper water layers are therefore completely cut off from the Marmara and Mediterranean Seas.

Although the Black Sea and the Sea of Japan are both highly enclosed, there is a crucial difference between them. Unlike the Sea of Japan, the Black Sea does not have a mechanism that generates dense surface water to drive downwelling. Therefore, there is almost no vertical mixing between the surface and deeper water layers.

In Black Sea surface waters, photosynthetic organisms can still produce the oxygen needed to support productive fisheries. In deeper waters, however, this oxygen is rapidly consumed by the decomposition of organic matter. In the Black Sea below a depth of about 150 m, oxygen concentrations fall to zero and aerobic (oxygen-consuming) organisms cannot survive. Moreover, in the absence of oxygen, the decomposition of organic matter relies on the reduction of sulfate ions (SO_4^{2-}), which generates large amounts of toxic hydrogen sulfide (H_2S) gas as a chemical byproduct. In this "bathtub," a casual dive to the bottom could have grave consequences.

Studies of seabed sediments in the Sea of Japan have revealed a period in the past when conditions there were very similar to those in

~~~~~~~~~~~~~~~~~~~~ *Column 1* ~~~~~~~~~~~~~~~~~~~~

the Black Sea today. This was about 20,000 years ago, during the peak of the last ice age. At the time, the growth of glaciers had substantially lowered sea levels, meaning that the Tsushima Strait was almost entirely dry. This drastically reduced the inflow of the Tsushima Warm Current into the Sea of Japan, reducing surface salinity and shutting down the thermohaline circulation.

As in the Black Sea, this interrupted the supply of oxygen to deep water and wiped out most biological activity at depth. What brought the Sea of Japan back from this "dead" state and restored it to its present form? When the ice age ended, the melting of the glaciers raised sea levels and recreated the Tsushima Strait, allowing the flow of the Tsushima Warm Current to increase.

You will learn more about this event that dramatically altered the Sea of Japan in chapter 4.

The Sea of Japan Is a Miniature Version of the Global Oceans

Although the Sea of Japan is only a small marginal sea bounded by the Eurasian continent and the Japanese archipelago, you would be wrong to think its importance is proportional to its size on a world map.

The interior of the Sea of Japan features an active deep-water circulation driven by the north-westerly winter monsoon. This circulation is completely self-contained within the Sea of Japan. The mechanisms that drive it are identical to those of the large-scale thermohaline circulation system (i.e., the "ocean conveyor belt") that spans the globe.

The Sea of Japan may be tiny, but the processes at work in it are the same as those in the global oceans.

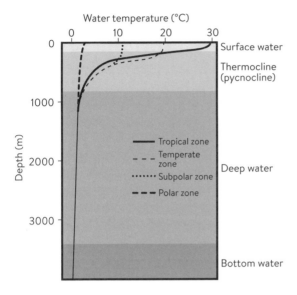

FIGURE 2–1: Typical classification scheme for oceanic depth zones. Lines indicate general patterns in water temperature by depth in different climatic zones, and shading indicates locations of the surface water, thermocline (or pycnocline), deep water, and bottom water, respectively.

2-1
Where Does the "Shallow Sea" End and the "Deep Sea" Begin?

In this chapter, I will reexamine the Sea of Japan in the broader context of the global oceans. Let's begin with some basics about water movement (i.e., circulation) in the oceans as a whole.

Typically, low-density (i.e., lighter) seawater is found on top of higher-density (i.e., heavier) seawater. In fluid mechanics terms, this is a "stratified structure" and is inherently stable. In the absence of external forces, the lighter surface water and heavier deep water cannot switch places. For example, in a bathtub, even when heat is applied from the bottom, heated (and therefore less dense) water rises to the surface, leaving lukewarm water below. Unless you were to apply a force by stirring the water with your hand, it will stay this way forever. The same thing applies to the oceans.

In oceanography, water that is close to the surface is called "surface water," and water at depth is called "deep water." Because deep water is heavy, the lighter surface water floats on top. Between the surface and deep water, there is an intermediate layer where temperature declines rapidly with depth (i.e., density increases with depth): this is called the "thermocline" (or "pycnocline").

The actual depths of the surface and deep-water layers are not strictly defined. Generally, in the open ocean, where the total water depth might be about 5000 m, the surface-water layer extends from the surface to a depth of about 50–100 m, and the deep-water layer extends from a depth of about 1000 m to the seafloor (fig. 2-1).

Sometimes, the deep-water layer may include a layer near the seabed called "bottom water." As with the other layers, this bottom water also is not strictly defined based on depth but is only considered to be present when there is a clear boundary in the temperature or salinity of the deep-water layer.

In any case, these ocean layers, which all together span several thousand meters in depth, are too large for anybody to stir by hand as you might do in your bathtub. However, as I discussed in chapter 1, if the temperature of the lighter surface water declines due to contact with cold air, or if the formation of sea ice (which is almost completely composed of fresh water) causes excess salt to get left behind in the unfrozen seawater, then surface-water density will be increased. A large enough increase in density can overturn the stable, stratified structure of the ocean. In other words, high-density surface water will sink due to the action of gravity, leading to vertical mixing between surface and deep-water layers.

2-2
The Biggest Ocean Circulation System Operates on a 2000-Year Timescale

Consider the world's oceans. The cold polar regions (more specifically, within the Arctic and Antarctic Circles) are places where surface water can be cooled sufficiently to sink into the deep sea. The main places where this is known to occur are the Labrador Sea and the waters off Greenland in the far northern Atlantic Ocean, and the Weddell and Ross Seas along the Antarctic coastline.

High-density water that sinks in the North Atlantic is known as "North Atlantic Deep Water." This water mass slides down the continental slope to the deep ocean and flows southward through the Atlantic Ocean along a route that traces the contours of the seafloor. Similarly, high-density water generated in the Southern Ocean is known as "Antarctic Bottom Water." This water mass slides down the Antarctic continental slope and merges with a portion of the North Atlantic Deep Water while circling Antarctica in a clockwise direction. Some of this water branches off to enter the Indian and Pacific Oceans and drifts northward through the deepest portions of each ocean basin. In each case, the flow of bottom water is pushed westward by the rotation of the earth.

These bottom water masses eventually rise back to the surface, merging with surface currents that return either to the North Atlantic or to the Southern Ocean off Antarctica. Having arrived where it all started, the water is cooled and sinks once more . . . and the whole process repeats.

The famous American chemical oceanographer Wallace Broecker (1931–2019) developed an easy-to-understand schematic diagram of this whole-ocean circulation pattern (fig. 2-2). Known as "Broecker's conveyor belt," this diagram is featured in nearly every textbook on oceanography. Keep in mind, however, that figure 2-2 is a simplification: in reality, there are no sustained belt-like currents that pass straight through the middle of ocean basins. Instead, the ocean-conveyor-belt concept expresses what you would observe if you averaged water movements over a prolonged period. Other researchers have proposed more complex conveyor-belt diagrams that more closely approximate the real ocean.

As I will discuss in detail in a later section, analyses of seawater radionuclides have shown that the ocean conveyor belt shown in figure 2-2 takes a very long time, around 1000–2000 years, to complete one circuit through the world's oceans.

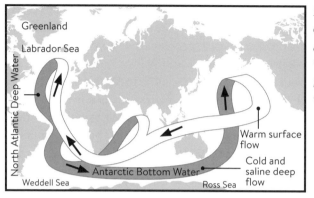

FIGURE 2–2:
Conceptual diagram of the "ocean conveyor belt" proposed by Wallace Broecker.

≈

2-3
The Sea of Japan Has Its Own "Miniature Circulation"

The above discussion of an ocean circulation pattern that starts with the sinking of heavy surface water may have reminded some of you of section 1-5-2, where I described a process known as thermohaline circulation that occurs in the Sea of Japan. If so, your intuition was spot on. In fact, a vast thermohaline circulation seamlessly connects all of the world's oceans (fig. 2-2). This global thermohaline circulation does not involve the Sea of Japan. As I stated in chapter 1, because the Sea of Japan is highly enclosed, it cannot take in deep water from other seas or oceans. However, the thermohaline circulation that operates within the small volume of the Sea of Japan is exactly the same in principle as what is shown in figure 2-2.

To summarize section 1-5-2, cold winter monsoon winds originating in Siberia strongly cool the surface water of the Sea of Japan and drive evaporation and ice formation in its northern and northwestern reaches; in this way, cold, highly saline, high-density surface water is generated. When this heavy surface water sinks due to the action of gravity, it drives an independent thermohaline circulation system (i.e., an ocean conveyor belt) that is contained solely within the boundaries of the Sea of Japan. In other words, when it comes to thermohaline circulation, the Sea of Japan is similar to the much larger global oceans.

In fact, figure 1-7 depicts the Sea of Japan's own version of the ocean conveyor belt. However, the scale of this conveyor belt is much smaller than that of the global oceans shown in figure 2-2. This is why the Sea of Japan is known as a miniature version of the global oceans, or a "miniature ocean."

The motion of the ocean conveyor belt is strongly reflected in the distribution of dissolved substances. In this section, I will focus on two representative substances: dissolved oxygen (O_2) gas and carbon-14 (also written ^{14}C), which is a radioisotope.

Oxygen gas is crucial for all land animals, including humans, and accounts for about 21% of atmospheric gas. Oxygen gas is also carried in its dissolved form in seawater, which makes it available for use by marine organisms.

In shallow waters, oxygen is produced by seagrasses, macroalgae, and invisible microorganisms known as phytoplankton. Like trees, they contain chlorophyll and use solar energy to photosynthesize, thereby converting inorganic compounds into organic matter (such as their own tissues). Oxygen gas is produced as a byproduct of this process.

Well-lit surface waters all around the world are rich in oxygen thanks to the action of photosynthesis. Surface-water oxygen concentrations are determined almost exclusively by oxygen solubility, which is in turn determined by water temperature and salinity. In other words, most surface water is saturated with oxygen. When oxygen-saturated surface water becomes heavier and sinks, it carries its dissolved oxygen into the deep ocean.

Incidentally, only the shallowest layers of the ocean receive enough sunlight for photosynthesis. This is because sunlight is quickly absorbed by water molecules (H_2O) and photosynthetic pigments or scattered by small floating particles and organisms. In other words, although sunlight abounds near the surface, the ocean rapidly darkens with depth.

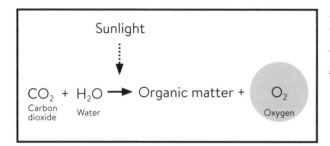

FIGURE 2-3:
The production
of oxygen gas by
photosynthesis.

In my youth, I took several deep-sea submersible dives to conduct research in the Sea of Japan as well as in the open ocean. Looking downward out the submersible's observation window, I could see that the ocean was completely dark at and below a depth of about 200 m. Because this darkness continues all the way to the sea floor, you can't see anything without the aid of powerful lights.

Photosynthesis cannot occur in darkness. Therefore, there is no oxygen production in the deep sea. Meanwhile, small organic particles constantly rain down from the surface into the deep ocean. These particles originate in dead organisms or in waste products excreted by living organisms. When illuminated by the lights of a submersible, these organic particles glow white and look exactly like fluttering, falling snowflakes. This is why they are known by the somewhat fanciful name of "marine snow."

Much of this marine snow is decomposed at depth by aerobic microorganisms in a process that consumes dissolved oxygen. This is the reverse of the reaction shown in figure 2-3. In the absence of some oxygen-supplying process, this reaction would reduce the oxygen concentration in the deep sea until there was no more oxygen left. Without oxygen, most organisms would be unable to survive. The Black Sea, which I discussed in column 1, is an example of a sea in which oxygen is absent below the surface water.

2-4
How Oxygen Is Delivered to the Deep Ocean

In the actual ocean, however, oxygen concentrations in deep water almost nowhere fall to zero. Although concentrations vary by region, the deep ocean generally contains at least 50% of the oxygen concentration at the surface because of a mechanism that counteracts the microbial consumption of oxygen by delivering fresh oxygen there. This mechanism is none other than thermohaline circulation, which drives vertical mixing. When surface water sinks, its abundant oxygen stores are transported to deep water.

Therefore, the oxygen gas produced in the surface waters of the Arctic and Southern Oceans is transported into the deep sea on the ocean conveyor belt, which then moves that oxygen throughout the global oceans. The farther downstream the water travels on the ocean conveyor belt, the lower the oxygen concentration becomes; this is because, as I mentioned earlier, while photosynthesis does not occur in the deep sea, the decomposition of organic matter (e.g., marine snow) continues to consume oxygen. This can be seen by comparing deep-sea oxygen concentrations from around the world. Figure 2-4 shows dissolved-oxygen concentrations measured at depths of 4000 m or more across the world's oceans. As I will explain in chapter 3, oxygen concentration measurements in seawater can be performed relatively easily aboard a ship. Consequently, a large trove of oxygen data has been accumulated from around the world. In figure 2-4, you can see that oxygen concentrations are quite high (260 µmol/kg) in the North Atlantic, where the ocean conveyor belt begins, but gradually decline to around 220 µmol/kg in the South Atlantic and the southern Indian Ocean, 200 µmol/kg in the South Pacific, and 160 µmol/kg in the North Pacific. In other words, the concentration declines as you go along the path of the conveyor belt shown in figure 2-2. Conversely, by tracing the direction in which oxygen concentrations decline, we can infer the path of the ocean conveyor belt.

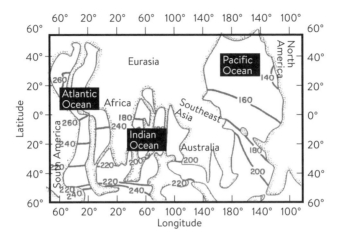

FIGURE 2-4: *Oxygen concentrations in μmol/kg of seawater in the global oceans below a depth of 4000 m (modified from Broecker and Peng, 1982). The unit micromole (abbreviation μmol) is a measure of the amount of a substance. A μmol is a millionth of a mole. A mole of oxygen gas (O₂) weighs 32 g.*

2-5
The Sea of Japan Is Rich in Oxygen

We have now seen how dissolved-oxygen concentrations in seawater are a very useful indicator of the path of the global ocean thermohaline circulation. Now let's return to the subject of the Sea of Japan. As with the global oceans, we would expect the thermohaline circulation in the Sea of Japan (see fig. 1-7) to transport surface oxygen to deep water. What, then, do you think a dissolved-oxygen profile of the Sea of Japan should look like?

Figure 2-5 shows a typical dissolved-oxygen concentration profile in the Sea of Japan. For comparison, I have also plotted an oxygen profile from a point in the western North Pacific that is located on the opposite side of the Japanese archipelago and at nearly the same latitude (40°N). As discussed in chapter 1, because the Sea of Japan and the western

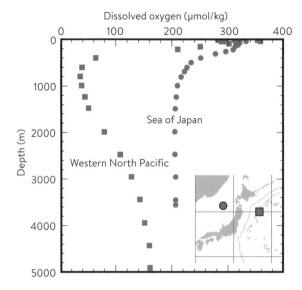

Figure 2-5:
Comparison of
dissolved-oxygen
concentrations in
the Sea of Japan and
the western North
Pacific. The inset
on the bottom right
shows the sampling
location for each
profile.

North Pacific are separated by the topographic barrier of the Japanese archipelago, there is no deep-water exchange between them. Consequently, their dissolved-oxygen profiles are very different. In fact, we can see that the Sea of Japan contains much more oxygen at depth.

The dissolved oxygen in the deep waters of the western North Pacific originates in the remote Southern Ocean. High-density surface waters in the cold Southern Ocean sink to form Antarctic Bottom Water, which travels northward though the South Pacific to eventually reach the North Pacific. By the time this water approaches Japan, it has had to traverse nearly the entire length of the Pacific Ocean from south to north over a period of many centuries. (According to radiocarbon-based measurements that I will describe in the next section, this is estimated to take about 500–1000 years.) During this whole period, dissolved-oxygen concentrations are continually reduced by ongoing organic-matter decomposition without being replenished by new oxygen input.

By contrast, the dissolved oxygen in the deep waters of the Sea of Japan originates nearby in the surface waters of the northern Sea of Japan itself.

Therefore, relatively little time has passed since the oxygen-rich surface water first sank into the deep sea. This means that only a small amount of oxygen has been consumed due to organic-matter decomposition, and the concentration of the remaining oxygen is much higher than that in the deep waters of the Pacific at an equivalent latitude.

≈

2-6
How Do You Measure the "Age" of Seawater?

Although dissolved-oxygen concentrations can be used to determine whether one sample of deep ocean water is older or newer than another sample, it cannot provide an estimate in years. How can we determine the age of a seawater sample, that is, the number of years that have passed since it first sank from the surface water into the deep ocean?

Fortunately, there is a substance that provides an optimal "stopwatch" for determining the age of seawater. The substance in question is a radio-isotope, more specifically a carbon isotope of mass 14 (also written as ^{14}C), which is known as "radiocarbon." The term radioisotope refers to a nuclide that spontaneously emits radiation, thereby converting itself to a different nuclide (this process is known as radioactive decay). The time it takes for the quantity of the first nuclide to decrease by half due to radioactive decay is known as the nuclide's "half-life." For radiocarbon, this time is 5730 years.

Figure 2-6 shows the principles behind ^{14}C dating. The nitrogen atoms (^{14}N) in the atmospheric nitrogen (N_2) undergo a nuclear reaction with thermal neutrons ("n" in fig. 2-6) derived from cosmic rays, producing ^{14}C. This ^{14}C is immediately oxidized to form carbon dioxide ($^{14}CO_2$), which then spreads uniformly throughout the atmosphere. A portion of this $^{14}CO_2$ also dissolves into the surface layers of the ocean. Because the rate at which ^{14}C is generated in the atmosphere remains essentially constant over time (strictly speaking, there are some fluctuations, but they are negligible), you can calculate the elapsed time since a water sample

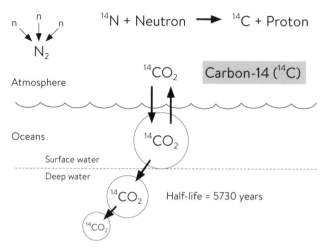

FIGURE 2–6: Basic principles used to determine the age of seawater.

was last in contact with the atmosphere (i.e., its "age") by examining how much the quantity of ^{14}C has decreased.

When you read the phrase "radiocarbon dating," many of you may have thought of its use in terrestrial archeology. Indeed, ^{14}C dating is often used to determine the age of materials excavated from ancient ruins. For example, suppose a piece of wood was excavated from the ruins of an ancient site. Wood contains ^{14}C in the form of cellulose. When the wood was part of a living tree, this tree would have continuously incorporated ^{14}C atoms from the atmosphere into cellulose. However, this supply of ^{14}C from the atmosphere would have stopped once the tree was cut down. From this time, the abundance of ^{14}C in the wood would have declined at a rate corresponding to its half-life of 5730 years. Suppose the abundance of ^{14}C in the excavated wood was half that of ^{14}C in the atmosphere. This would mean that the ancient ruins were likely in use about 5730 years ago.

≋

2-7

Seawater as Old as the Birth of Christ

Let's bring the subject back to the ocean. The ocean surface constantly exchanges carbon dioxide with the atmosphere, meaning that surface-water ^{14}C levels are always in equilibrium with atmospheric ^{14}C. However, if the surface water becomes heavier and sinks into deep water, it can no longer exchange carbon dioxide with the atmosphere, meaning that ^{14}C levels will decline at a rate corresponding to its half-life (fig. 2-6). Therefore, by measuring ^{14}C concentrations in deep seawater from around the world, researchers can determine whether the seawater is old or new (i.e., how many years have passed since the water sank and lost contact with the atmosphere).

This is precisely the process that was used to create the diagram of the ocean conveyor belt shown in figure 2-2. What's more, radiocarbon dating was also used to show that the time needed for a parcel of seawater to travel once through the entire conveyor belt is roughly 1000–2000 years. In other words, seawater that first sank in the North Atlantic around the time of the birth of Christ is now, some 2000 years later, reaching the North Pacific on the eastern side of the Japanese archipelago. In those same 2000 years, human societies have been involved in a truly mind-boggling array of activities. (In fact, I can remember being overwhelmed by the number of world events I had to learn in history class at school.) Throughout all of these 2000 action-packed years of human history, in the depths of the ocean and unseen by human eyes, the thermohaline circulation has slowly, slowly inched forward and is only now completing one circuit around the earth.

2-8

The "Miniature Ocean" Is a Canary in a Coal Mine: What Comes Next for the Sea of Japan?

How long does it take for the Sea of Japan's "miniature" conveyor belt to complete one circuit?

Researchers have also used radiocarbon to measure the age of deep water in the Sea of Japan. I will save the details for chapter 3, but if we skip to the conclusion here, I can tell you that the estimated timescale is 100–200 years. Nearly identical results have also been obtained by measuring the concentration of other radionuclides and man-made chemicals.

In other words, the Sea of Japan's thermohaline circulation is one order of magnitude faster than that of the global oceans. During the 2000 years since the birth of Christ, the deep water of the Sea of Japan has been replaced by surface water some 10–20 times.

One of the questions I am most interested in is how the Sea of Japan, as a miniature version of the global oceans, will respond to ongoing global environmental changes caused by human activities. After all, the fact that the timescale of thermohaline circulation in the Sea of Japan is just one-tenth that of the global oceans suggests that the Sea of Japan is much more sensitive to global environmental change.

How can we detect the impacts of global environmental change in the Sea of Japan before they become apparent in the global oceans? This question is drawing strong interest not only from oceanographers in Japan but also from those in countries near and far, including in the West.

As you will read in the column at the end of this chapter, oceanographers from three countries (Japan, South Korea, and Russia) located along the Sea of Japan coast have teamed up to launch a joint international research program called "Circulation Research of the East Asian Marginal Seas (CREAMS)" to study the Sea of Japan as its first target. This venture has also been joined by researchers from China, Germany, and the United States. Together, these researchers are continuing to undertake comprehensive studies of the physical, chemical, and biological oceanography of the Sea of Japan.

The Oceanography Society, an international oceanographic organization based in the United States, even published a special issue of its magazine *Oceanography* in 2006 on the Sea of Japan that introduced to a broad audience the CREAMS project and other research conducted in the Sea of Japan. The importance of continued observations in the Sea of Japan is reiterated throughout the special issue. This is because what is about to happen in the Sea of Japan may be a sign of what's to come for the rest of the world.

Historically, coal miners carried bird cages containing live canaries into mines. If a canary suddenly stopped singing, the miners would understand that the conditions had become dangerous and would retreat back to safety. Canaries are sensitive to toxic gasses such as methane and carbon monoxide: when concentrations of these gasses rise in a mine, canaries can quickly detect the change in conditions.

The sensitivity of the Sea of Japan to global environmental change is analogous to the role that canaries once played in coal mines. In fact, subtle changes in the chemical properties of seawater in the Sea of Japan are already beginning to become detectable. In chapter 6, I will talk in detail about how the Sea of Japan is sounding the alarm for the globe.

~~~~~~~~~~~~~~~~~~~~~~~~~~ *Column 2* ~~~~~~~~~~~~~~~~~~~~~~~~~~

The CREAMS Project: A Research Project by Countries That Border the Sea of Japan

The United Nations Convention on the Law of the Sea (ratified in 1982, implemented in 1994) defined the boundaries of various exclusive economic zones (EEZs) across the world's oceans. Japan, which is surrounded by oceans, has a vast EEZ. In fact, the overall marine area under Japanese administration (including territorial waters) totals some 4.47 million km^2. This places Japan's EEZ as the sixth largest in the world.

Although an EEZ is generally defined as extending 200 nautical miles (about 370 km) offshore of a nation's coastline, if this area overlaps with a similar area extending offshore of the coastline of another country, an intermediate boundary must be agreed upon by both parties. For this reason, the Sea of Japan is divided between the EEZs of Japan, South Korea, North Korea, and Russia. Researchers from each country must obtain government consent to conduct oceanographic research within the EEZ of another country.

Although Japanese oceanographers had previously been in close contact with researchers from South Korea and from what was then known as the Soviet Union, the establishment of EEZs has further emphasized the importance of international cooperation. With the end of the Cold War in 1989, there was growing enthusiasm among countries along the Sea of Japan to participate in joint research projects.

In 1993, the Grants-in-Aid for Scientific Research Program, which was administered at the time by the Japanese Ministry of Education, launched an international scientific research project headed by Professor Masaki Takematsu, then a faculty member at Kyushu University. This was the CREAMS project, a joint effort by researchers from Japan, South Korea, and Russia to carry out oceanographic research over almost the entire Sea of Japan. The Russian research vessel *Professor Khromov* was

~~~~~~

~~~~~~~~~~~~~~~~~~~~~~~ *Column 2* ~~~~~~~~~~~~~~~~~~~~~~~

the platform for research cruises.

Researchers from China, Germany, and the United States have also joined the effort, and the CREAMS project has contributed substantially to our knowledge of the physics, chemistry, and biology of the Sea of Japan. In 2005, an advisory panel for the CREAMS program was established within the North Pacific Marine Science Organization (PICES, whose members include Canada, China, Japan, Russia, South Korea, and the United States), and the program's focus has since expanded beyond the Sea of Japan to include ongoing joint research projects in the East China Sea.

The Sea of Japan Has Its Own Distinct Water Mass! Explorations of the Bathtub's Depths

In the 1930s, Japanese oceanographers embarked on a full-fledged effort to study the waters of the Sea of Japan from its surface to its deepest depths. This effort revealed that the interior of the "bathtub" known as the Sea of Japan contains a large and unique water mass (dubbed "Japan Sea Proper Water") that is extraordinarily cold, and rich in oxygen.

The late 1970s saw the adoption of cutting-edge research tools such as high-precision CTDs (Conductivity, Temperature, and Depth sensors) and radionuclide dating techniques. The results drove important advances in our understanding of the Sea of Japan, including the discovery of an extremely uniform bottom-water layer and the first calculations of the time scale of its thermohaline circulation.

3-1
Pioneering Explorers of the Sea of Japan

Most of the scientific information about the Sea of Japan that you will learn in this book was obtained within a relatively short time period, namely the past 100 years. Prior to this, although the Sea of Japan was extremely important for trade, it was rarely the subject of scientific exploration or research. In fact, the very idea of pursuing a scientific understanding of the Sea of Japan did not take root in any of its neighboring countries until fairly recently.

However, in the late eighteenth and early nineteenth centuries, several pioneers from Russia and Western Europe successfully sailed frigates and warships into the Sea of Japan. These were, in 1787, France's Jean-François de La Pérouse; in 1796, Britain's William Robert Broughton; and in 1805, Russia's Ivan Fyodorovich Kruzenshtern. These first explorers mapped the Sea of Japan and gained a rough understanding of its bathymetry and currents.

La Pérouse's fleet of two frigates first entered the Sea of Japan via the Tsushima Strait on 25 May 1787. A map appended to *Voyage de La Pérouse Autour du Monde* (The Voyage of La Pérouse around the World), published in 1797, shows how the fleet proceeded eastward along the southeast coast of South Korea and through the Sea of Japan until it reached the waters offshore of the Noto Peninsula, where it changed course to the northwest and voyaged northward along the Russian coastline (fig. 3-1). In this map, the name of the Sea of Japan is given as *Mer du Japon* (the Sea of Japan).

This name had already been used by the French cartographer G.R. de Vaugondy in his 1750 map entitled *L'Empire du Japon* (The Japanese Empire). Therefore, La Pérouse may have simply borrowed the name from his compatriot.

La Pérouse very nearly reached the Strait of Tartary (it would not be formally discovered until several years later, in 1808–09, by Denjuro Matsuda and Rinzo Mamiya), and seemed all but convinced of the strait's existence (the name *Manche de Tartarie* [Strait of Tartary] even appears on the

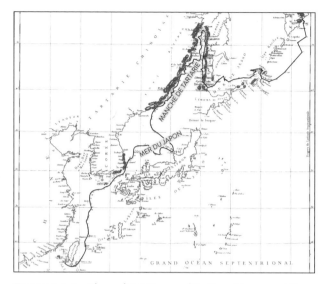

FIGURE 3-1: *La Pérouse's 1797 map of the Sea of Japan and the Japanese archipelago. The black line shows his route through the Sea of Japan (from* Voyage de La Pérouse Autour du Monde *pt. 16–22, translated by Tadao Kobayashi). The route and several place names are shown in bold for emphasis.*

map shown in fig. 3-1). However, either because of bad weather or insufficient depth, he was forced to turn back before passing through the strait.

He then proceeded into the Sea of Okhotsk through the La Pérouse Strait before reaching the Port of Petropavlovsk-Kamchatsky on the Kamchatka Peninsula.

3-2
Who Named the Sea of Japan?

When Russia's Kruzenshtern embarked on his voyage into the Sea of

Japan, he sailed with Nikolai Rezanov, the Russian Ambassador to Japan, who had been tasked with establishing Russo-Japanese trade relations. They sailed westward along the southern coast of the Japanese archipelago before reaching the Port of Nagasaki in October 1804. Despite being made to wait in Nagasaki for six months, their proposal to establish trade relations was rejected by the shogunate. From Nagasaki, they then proceeded into the Sea of Japan. As with La Pérouse, they transited through the Sea of Okhotsk to reach the Port of Petropavlovsk-Kamchatsky.

Kruzenshtern's report on his voyages, *Reise um die Welt* (Journey around the World), includes a world map in which the Sea of Japan is indicated by the name *море Японское* (Sea of Japan). Kruzenshtern's naming may have been based on La Pérouse's earlier account, but this has not been confirmed.

Both La Pérouse's and Kruzenshtern's accounts were read around the world and led to the widespread popularization of the name "Sea of Japan." Of course, the name had in fact first appeared in maps published by other Western mapmakers. In addition to the previously mentioned de Vaugondy, an even earlier example is the use of *Mare Japonicum* (Sea of Japan) in Italy in a 1617 map of Japan by C. Blancus (Nakano, 2015). However, I am inclined to credit La Pérouse, and secondarily Kruzenshtern, for coining the name. These two figures not only explored the Sea of Japan from end to end, but also conducted pioneering oceanographic research and thoroughly documented their voyages in their respective reports.

Yet this coinage at first received almost no recognition in Japan, which at the time was firmly in the grip of its isolationist *sakoku* policy. In fact, the Japanese people had no history of naming seas or oceans in general, and on the few occasions when the Sea of Japan needed to be referred to by name, it was often called *Hokkai* (North Sea) because of its location along the northern coastline of the archipelago. Similarly, Korean sources have used the name *Donghae* (East Sea) because of the Sea of Japan's location along the eastern coastline of the Korean peninsula; this name remains in use today. The name *Nihonkai* (Sea of Japan) only began to appear in Japanese maps after the 1860s, and it is clear that the name was imported from the West.

La Perouse's account of his voyage contains many interesting anecdotes. I will recount a few that relate to the Sea of Japan in the column at the end of chapter 5.

≈

3-3
Russian Scientists Pioneered the Scientific Study of the Sea of Japan

In the late nineteenth century, the Russian state actively sought to expand its territory along its southern border. Having gained control of the northwestern coastline of the Sea of Japan (the Primorskaya Oblast) through the Treaty of Aigun in 1858 and the Convention of Beijing in 1860, the government immediately dispatched the warship *Posadnik* to Aso Bay in the Tsushima Islands in 1861 in an effort to occupy it by force (this is known as the Tsushima Incident). Their aim was to secure a strategic outpost (a warm-water port) to provide access into the Pacific Ocean through the Sea of Japan, but after encountering combined resistance from the Tsushima Domain, the Japanese shogunate, and the British Navy, they were forced to retreat after six months. (The British government is thought to have seen the Tsushima Islands as a key bulwark against expanding Russian influence.)

Following this setback, the Russian Navy hastened the development of a military port in Vladivostok and continued to conduct observations of the Sea of Japan. For example, L.I. Schrenck published research papers summarizing these observations in 1870 and 1874. These papers included information on water temperature, density, and currents. The names I used in chapter 1 for the Sea of Japan's principle currents, such as the Tsushima Warm Current and the Liman Cold Current, were first established in Schrenck's papers.

Admiral Stepan O. Makarov is mainly known for having served as commander of the Russian Pacific Fleet in Lüshun from the start of the Russo-Japanese War (1904–05) until his death when his ship was sunk by a Japanese mine. However, he was also an excellent oceanographer. In 1894, he authored an extensive report that compiled the results of oceanographic research conducted aboard the warship *Vityaz* in the Sea of Japan and the Pacific Ocean.

When conducting naval operations, a good understanding of ocean currents and weather is essential. In Japan, a particularly famous forecast for the Sea of Japan ("Clear weather expected but waves to remain high") was issued by Takematsu Okada, Director of the Central Meteorological Observatory, on 26 May 1905 just before a decisive naval battle in the Russo-Japanese War. During World War II, several excellent oceanographers with doctorates in scientific disciplines were also members of the Japanese military. These include Colonel Saburo Kishindo, who led meteorological and oceanographic observations at the Japanese Navy's Hydrographic Department, and Colonel Toshio Akiyoshi, who conducted observations for tidal monitoring and celestial navigation.

3-4
The Japanese Scientist Who Used over 10,000 Bottles to Study Ocean Currents

Although Russia pioneered the early oceanography of the Sea of Japan, its defeat in the Russo-Japanese War and the subsequent onset of the Russian Revolution (1917) severely curtailed further research efforts. Instead, the next era of research was led by Japanese oceanographers.

Japan pursued an intense program of westernization after the Meiji Restoration of 1868. This not only boosted the academic rigor of Japanese oceanographers but also emphasized the urgent need to adopt internationally recognized oceanographic techniques. Researchers were called upon to quickly collect detailed oceanographic data from across the Japanese archipelago to serve the needs of coastal fisheries and maritime defense. In particular, the Sea of Japan was likely deemed a top research priority because of the presence of various foreign countries on its opposite shore.

Up to this point, our understanding of the surface currents and bathymetry of the Sea of Japan owed much to explorers such as La Pérouse and his successors, as well as to Russian pioneers such as Schrenck and Makarov. Additionally, drift bottle experiments conducted by Japan's Yuji Wada (1859–1918) had also produced enormously important results.

Wada was one of the fathers of Japanese oceanography. He graduated from Tokyo Imperial University and worked at the Home Ministry's Geographic Bureau before joining the Central Meteorological Observatory in 1893. Here, he conducted oceanographic observations and, despite a lack of understanding from his colleagues, began using drift bottles to study ocean currents. In 1913–17, while serving as director of the Incheon Meteorological Observatory, he released some 13,357 drift bottles (of which 2990 were recovered) in the waters around Japan. His surface-current data resulting from these painstakingly collected bottles were published in 1922 in the *Nihon Kankai Kairyu Chosa Jisseki* (Surface-Current Data from the Waters around Japan).

Yet in contrast to this intensive research into surface currents, the depths of the Sea of Japan remained almost entirely overlooked by oceanographers. What are some properties of the water at depths of several hundred to several thousand meters, and what is the distribution of temperature, salinity, and other major chemical components? Even these sorts of fundamental questions went completely unaddressed until the late 1920s.

3-5
How to Collect Water Samples from Multiple Depths at Once

As I mentioned in the prologue, the chemical composition of seawater contains important clues needed to explain numerous phenomena that occur on the earth and in the oceans in particular. To find these clues, it is first necessary to collect seawater samples and analyze their

FIGURE 3-2:
Nansen bottles in
use (photographs
courtesy of Hiroshi
Hasumoto).

chemistry. For surface water, the sampling procedure can be as simple as scooping water into a bucket or some other container. For water at depths of several hundred to several thousand meters however, this is clearly insufficient. Instead, what is needed is a purpose-built water-sampling device that includes a sampling container with a built-in mechanism to open and close watertight lids. This apparatus is then attached to a cable and lowered into the ocean in a very labor-intensive process.

In the early twentieth century, the Norwegian oceanographer Fridtjof Nansen constructed an excellent water-sampling device; this device is called the "Nansen bottle" (fig. 3-2) in his honor. The Nansen bottle consists of opening/closing mechanisms attached to both the top and bottom of a metal, cylindrical container with a water capacity of around 2 L. At the appropriate depth, the container is rotated 180° to seal off the top and bottom, thereby isolating the water sample inside. Because of this rotational movement, the Nansen bottle is also known in Japan as a *tentoshiki saisuiki* (tumbling water sampler). By arranging a number of these samplers at different locations along a cable and lowering them into the ocean,

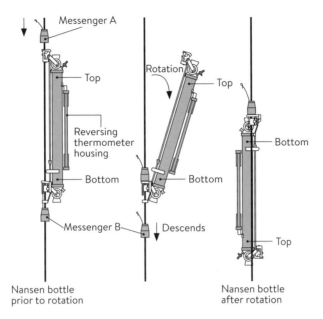

FIGURE 3–3: How Nansen bottles are used to collect water samples. The first messenger weight (Messenger A) triggers rotation of the Nansen bottle, which seals the water sample within the bottle. At the same time, the second messenger weight (Messenger B) slides down the cable to repeat the process with the next Nansen bottle (figure modified from Defant, 1961).

it is possible to collect seawater samples from multiple depths at once.

To seal off the water sample, a metal weight called a "messenger" is slid down the cable (fig. 3-3). When the first messenger (Messenger A) collides with the top of the shallowest Nansen bottle on the cable, the connection between the top of the bottle and the cable is disengaged and the bottle flips under its own weight. This motion not only isolates the seawater sample, but also triggers the descent of a second messenger (Messenger B) that will slide down to the next bottle on the cable and so forth until the deepest Nansen bottle on the cable has flipped.

Nansen bottles have contributed greatly to the field of oceanography. They were at one time an indispensable tool for deep seawater collection, and remain in use today.

However, these bottles also have several disadvantages; for example, their metal construction makes them unsuitable for trace-metal studies and they cannot be used to collect large water volumes of 10–20 L. Plastic water samplers such as Niskin bottles and Go-Flo devices, which use springs or elastic bands to seal and unseal the sample container, do not have these disadvantages. Therefore, they are increasingly in use today.

3-6
How to Take Accurate Depth Measurements: Exploits in Glasswork

Incidentally, accurate measurements of water temperature and depth are fundamental for almost all seawater studies. For example, water temperature is needed to calculate seawater density. In the earliest era of oceanographic observation, researchers tried to measure water temperature by quickly inserting a thermometer into the water-sampling device after it had been hauled back aboard the ship. However, even if the water-sampling device had been built with an insulated exterior, measurements obtained by this method inevitably deviated somewhat from the actual temperature in the ocean. The greater the depth of the water sample, the larger the deviation was likely to be. Although this source of error was well known, oceanographers struggled for many years to develop a more accurate system for temperature measurement.

What about depth measurements? If you put distance markings on the cable holding the water samplers, you can roughly determine the depth of the samplers. However, this method is also fraught with inaccuracies. For example, the cable is unlikely to hang straight down. If the research ship is being pushed by something (e.g., an ocean current, wind, or both) the cable will be pulled sideways by the horizontal motion of the ship. In

FIGURE 3–4:
*Reversing
thermometers.
Unprotected (left)
and protected
(right) varieties.
The length of each
thermometer is
about 32 cm.*

this situation, even if you knew that you had lowered 100 m of cable into the water, the actual depth of the bottom of the cable would be less than 100 m. Moreover, there is no way to know from the ship how much shallower the true depth might be. This seems like an intractable problem.

However, a solution was in fact invented in the form of a highly useful thermometer that can accurately measure temperature and depth at the precise location of the water sampler when the sample is isolated. This special thermometer uses mercury to measure temperature and has a unique glass construction. When the orientation of the thermometer is reversed underwater, the mercury column splits into two parts, and the relative proportion of the mercury column that splits off serves as a record of the temperature at the time of the reversal. Because of this reversing motion, this device is known as a "reversing thermometer" (fig. 3-4).

Two different types of reversing thermometers are used in tandem: one "unprotected" thermometer records higher temperatures at greater water pressures, and a second "protected" thermometer is unaffected by changing water pressure. The first thermometer can be used to accurately determine water pressure (i.e., depth), and the second records temperature. This setup was first manufactured in Britain in 1878, and dramatic improvements to the accuracy of the design were later achieved in Germany. Currently, the margin of error for temperature measurements with reversing thermometers is as low as ±0.01°C.

In Japan, production of these thermometers began around 1913, but initial models were quite inaccurate. A long and difficult process of innovation using proprietary manufacturing techniques culminated in the production around 1938 of Japanese reversing thermometers that were just as accurate as the German models.

These thermometers are attached to and undergo the same 180° rotation as the Nansen bottles. In this way, they store the information needed to determine the exact temperature and depth of the seawater sample.

The manufacture of accurate reversing thermometers necessitated all the ingenuity of skilled glassmakers. A novel by the famous Japanese novelist Jiro Nitta, *Garasu to Suigin* (Glass and Mercury), depicts the remarkable lives of the glassmakers who were obsessed with the production of accurate reversing thermometers.

However, as described in section 3-10, electronic sensors such as CTDs have undergone dramatic improvements in the accuracy of their temperature and pressure (i.e., depth) measurements. As a result, reversing thermometers have increasingly fallen out of use.

≈

3-7
An Oceanographic Survey Using 50 Ships at Once

The circumstances finally aligned for a full-scale research survey of the Sea of Japan in the late 1920s.

As Japan became more of a world power, it also accumulated the ships, research facilities, and onboard sampling equipment needed to conduct oceanographic surveys. At this time, two pioneering scientists made a series of new discoveries in the Sea of Japan.

First, Kanji Suda (1892–1976) of the Kobe Marine Meteorological Observatory surveyed the western Sea of Japan in 1928–30 using the 125-t research vessel *Shunpu Maru*. His survey was the first to collect and analyze the chemical composition of seawater from the Sea of Japan at depths below 1000 m.

Suda was born in Gunma Prefecture and graduated from Tohoku Imperial University. He joined the Kobe Marine Meteorological Observatory in 1921 and conducted his research in the Sea of Japan. Subsequently, he served as head of the Fukuoka branch of the Central Meteorological Observatory, and in 1946, he became director of the Maritime Safety Agency's Hydrographic Department. Then, in 1962–66, he served as director of the Tokai University School of Marine Science and Technology. In addition to his achievements in seismology and oceanography, he is also remembered for his research on cold-weather damage in the Tohoku region. His books include *Kaiyo Kagaku* (Marine Science) and *Kaiyo Butsurigaku* (Marine Physics).

Following on from Suda's work, a large-scale simultaneous survey of the Sea of Japan was conducted in 1932 mainly under the direction of Michitaka Uda (1905–82) of the Imperial Fisheries Experimental Station's Marine Research Department at the Ministry of Agriculture and Forestry.

Uda was born in Kochi Prefecture and graduated from Tokyo Imperial University. He joined the Fisheries Training Institute at the Ministry of Agriculture and Forestry in 1927 and directed intensive observations of the Sea of Japan. After World War II, he served as director of the Nagasaki Marine Meteorological Observatory and the Fisheries Agency's Tokai Fisheries Research Institute and was a professor at the Tokyo University of Fisheries and at Tokai University. He dedicated his career to the study and dissemination of knowledge about marine physics and fisheries oceanography. His books include *Kaiyogaku* (Oceanography), *Nihon no Umi* (The Oceans of Japan), and *Umi ni Ikite* (A Life of the Sea).

Uda's simultaneous observation program was a huge undertaking and involved approximately 50 research vessels. One of the most important of these was the Imperial Fisheries Experiment Station's *Soyo Maru* (built in 1925, displacement: 202 t), which was equipped with a winch capable of retrieving water samples from a depth of 3000 m. This ship extensively surveyed the main regions of the Sea of Japan by following a zigzag route that involved three round trips between the Eurasian continent and the Japanese archipelago. During this voyage, the researchers collected a large number of deep-water samples in Nansen bottles and analyzed their chemical composition; finally, it was at this time that the temperature and chemistry of the "bathtub" known as the Sea of Japan were fully revealed.

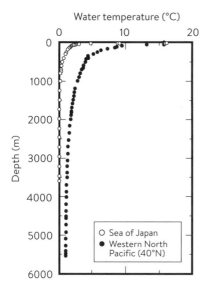

Water temperature (°C)

FIGURE 3-5: *The Sea of Japan features a steep decline in water temperature with depth. Data from the western North Pacific are shown for comparison. The latitude of both sampling locations is around 40°N. Although the temperature of the surface water (approximately 16°C) is nearly identical at the two locations, the temperature profiles at depth are completely different.*

≋

3-8
The Discovery of Japan Sea Proper Water

The observations conducted aboard the *Shunpu Maru* and *Soyo Maru* obtained truly fascinating results. First, it was discovered that the temperature of the Sea of Japan declines rapidly with depth and the water quickly becomes quite cold. Although seawater generally cools with depth in every ocean, in the Sea of Japan this temperature gradient is unusually steep. While the temperature of the surface water may be around 16°C, this drops to 1°C or less at a depth of 200–300 m and reaches almost 0°C at 1000 m. The temperature then remains nearly constant beyond this depth (fig. 3-5).

Chemical analysis demonstrated that the 0–1°C water mass located below 200–300 m depth is characterized by extremely high oxygen concentrations and a nearly uniform salinity. This is exactly what I described in section 2-5.

From this information, Suda formulated the following hypothesis in 1932: Cold and highly saline surface water forms along the northern coastline of the Sea of Japan in winter, and the sinking of this heavy surface water actively mixes the deep-water layer.

At the time, the concept of thermohaline circulation was not well established, and this was therefore a radical idea. Uda collected a large amount of data to support Suda's hypothesis, and coined the term "the water-mass proper to the Japan Sea" to describe the uniform water mass that is found below a depth of 200 m in the Sea of Japan (Uda, 1934). This name was later shortened to "Japan Sea Proper Water" and became internationally recognized in academic circles.

In the surface water, phytoplankton constantly produce oxygen as a byproduct of photosynthesis. Active vertical mixing of the ocean driven by surface-water downwelling then transports this abundant oxygen supply into the deep sea. Suda and Uda were some of the first to become aware of this process in the 1930s. This allowed them to discover the mechanisms behind the formation and persistence of the Sea of Japan's own deep water mass (Japan Sea Proper Water).

≈

3-9
The Three Subdivisions of Japan Sea Proper Water: The Key Was Water Depth

After the groundbreaking discovery of the Sea of Japan's own distinct water mass, Japanese observations of the Sea of Japan entered a period of stagnation due to the outbreak of World War II and Japan's eventual defeat in August 1945.

In 1948, some three years after the end of the war, the Maritime Safety Agency's Hydrographic Department used the research vessel *Kaiyo Maru* No. 4 (displacement: 200 t) to carry out observations of the Yamato Basin and the eastern part of the Japan Basin. In addition, beginning around

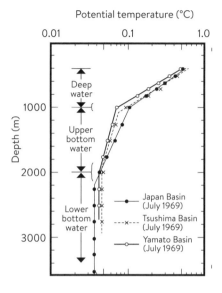

Potential temperature (°C)

FIGURE 3–6: *Water-temperature profiles showing the characteristics of Japan Sea Proper Water (modified from Nitani, 1972). The water-temperature data were collected in July 1969 by the Maritime Safety Agency's research vessel* Takuyo *at depths greater than 400 m. Each line shows a temperature profile obtained in one of the three basins of the Sea of Japan. Because the temperature differences are so slight, the x-axis is shown on a logarithmic scale. For an explanation of the term "potential temperature," please see the column at the end of this chapter.*

1960, the Japan Meteorological Agency's Maizuru Marine Meteorological Observatory became responsible for carrying out regular observations of the Sea of Japan. These observations took the form of quarterly cruises using vessels such as the *Kofu Maru* (displacement: 346 t) and *Seifu Maru* (355 t).

Hideo Nitani of the Japan Oceanographic Data Center used the enormous volume of data collected in the Sea of Japan between 1928 and 1971 to conduct cutting-edge analyses that revealed long-term fluctuations in the temperature, salinity, and dissolved-oxygen concentration of the Sea of Japan (Nitani, 1972). His article, which I read as a graduate student, was part of what inspired me to study the Sea of Japan.

As I described earlier, the temperature of Japan Sea Proper Water falls within the very narrow range of 0–1°C. However, since reversing thermometers have an accuracy of about ±0.01°C, careful measurements should be able to reveal temperature variations with depth even within this narrow 1°C range.

As shown in figure 3-6, in each of the three basins of the Sea of Japan, temperature gradually decreases with depth. A notable feature is the two clear shifts in the temperature–depth relationship at around 1000–1100 and 2000–2300 m.

Nitani believed that the two shifts must be related in some way to the circulation of Japan Sea Proper Water, and differentiated the water mass using these depth boundaries. In other words, he categorized the portion of the Japan Sea Proper Water shallower than 1000 m as deep water, the portion at 1000–2000 m as upper bottom water, and the deepest portion between 2000 m and the seabed as lower bottom water. In this way, he gradually began to differentiate the water layers that had been grouped together under the name of Japan Sea Proper Water at the time of their initial discovery.

≈

3-10
Using Technology to Visualize the Invisible

Several major technological innovations changed the landscape of ocean observation in the late 1970s. Foremost among these was the widespread use of field-based high-precision sensors known as CTDs. The C in CTD stands for conductivity; the electrical conductivity of seawater can be used to calculate salinity. T stands for temperature. Although D stands for depth, the device actually measures water pressure, which can be converted to depth.

Professor Yoshio Horibe (1923–2019), who oversaw my graduate research at the Ocean Research Institute at the University of Tokyo, was a pioneer who updated many traditional oceanographic protocols by adopting numerous new technologies.

This technological revolution in ocean observation made it possible to visualize what had previously been invisible. For example, during this time, Japanese researchers first gained access to a high-precision CTD (manufactured by Neil Brown Instrument Systems, USA) capable

FIGURE 3–7: *The first-generation research vessel (R/V)* Hakuho Maru *(displacement: 3226 t; operated by the University of Tokyo) was built in 1967 and operated until 1988. Currently, the second-generation* Hakuho Maru *(displacement: 3991 t) is operated by the Japan Agency for Marine-Earth Science and Technology (JAMSTEC) (see column at the end of chapter 6 for details).*

of measuring water temperature with a precision of ±0.0005°C, which vastly improved upon the precision of reversing thermometers.

Reversing thermometers attached to water-sampling devices can only obtain measurements from a limited number of depths, such as in steps of every 100 or 250 m. CTDs, on the other hand, collect data continuously as you move them up and down in the water column. Such precise and continuous depth profiles allow scientists to understand even small-scale variations in temperature.

The high-precision CTD was deployed in the Sea of Japan from aboard the University of Tokyo's research vessel *Hakuho Maru* (fig. 3-7, plate 2) in 1979. The data that were obtained from this cruise would eventually lead to exciting advances in our understanding of Japan Sea Proper Water.

≈

3-11
At Last, a Glimpse of the Sea of Japan's Deepest Reaches

The CTD was lowered to depths just above the seafloor in four locations in the Sea of Japan. At the time, I had just earned my doctorate, and I was assigned to transfer the huge trove of raw CTD data (stored as binary numbers) onto magnetic tape and use a minicomputer to convert them into human-readable values of temperature and salinity.

The data processing had progressed smoothly, and having finished calculating potential temperatures (a temperature measure that corrects for the increase in *in situ* [at the sampling depth] temperature at high water pressures; see the column at the end of this chapter for details), I was finally ready to plot the data. I plotted depth on the vertical axis and water temperature on the horizontal axis. At the time, no one had yet seen a high-resolution continuous temperature profile of Japan Sea Proper Water. To make sure I wouldn't miss even the slightest temperature shift, I zoomed in the horizontal axis to a range of just 0.1°C (from 0.03–0.13°C), and hit the enter key on my keyboard. This was it. What would I see next?

The instant I saw the plot (shown in fig. 3-8), I jumped with excitement. My reaction might sound excessive, but this was a historic moment: it was the first time that anyone in the world had seen the fine-scale temperature structure of the Sea of Japan.

The plot yielded two important revelations. One is that although water temperatures at 1000–2000 m gradually decrease with depth, below a depth of about 2200 m, water temperatures are so uniform that even the ±0.0005°C resolution of the CTD could not detect any changes with depth. The second revelation is that a boundary (i.e., a front or discontinuity) is present just above the uniform water temperature layer (this is indicated in fig. 3-8 by the bold arrow at around 2000 m).

This uniform temperature structure of the bottom water was observed not only in the eastern Japan Basin, but also in the Yamato and Tsushima Basins. Therefore, it appears that a cold water mass with vertically uniform temperature is found throughout the Sea of Japan at

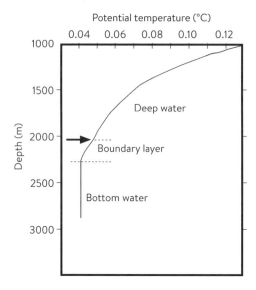

Potential temperature (°C)

FIGURE 3–8: *The fine-scale temperature structure of Japan Sea Proper Water. This potential temperature profile was obtained in July 1979 in the eastern Japan Basin (41°21'N, 137°20'E), and was the first vertical profile obtained using the high-precision CTD carried aboard the* Hakuho Maru. *The bold arrow indicates a front between deep and bottom water (modified from Gamo and Horibe, 1983).*

depths below 2000–2500 m. I decided to name this uniform water mass "Japan Sea Bottom Water." This is most likely the same water mass as what was termed "lower bottom water" in figure 3-6.

Normally, in the Pacific and other oceans, the temperature of bottom water continues to decrease with depth all the way to the seafloor at 5000 or 6000 m. However, the temperature of Japan Sea Bottom Water remains uniform. What could this possibly mean?

3-12
When Did the Bottom Water Sink?

In section 2-1, as an analogy, I described a scenario in which you might stir the water in a bathtub such that the hot surface and lukewarm bottom layers mix to create a uniform temperature across the entire tub. This analogy holds the key to solving the mystery of why Japan Sea

Bottom Water maintains a uniform temperature across a depth range of 1000 m. The fact of this uniform temperature over such a large depth range suggests that there is some internal process that actively stirs the water mass to achieve constant vertical mixing.

In the absence of such a process, the bottom water would gradually mix with the deep water above it and erase any discontinuities in the temperature profile. In other words, this would result in a smooth and continuous temperature decline with depth.

Japan Sea Bottom Water is the coldest and densest water mass in the Sea of Japan. Yet before it arrived at its present location, the water that would become Japan Sea Bottom Water must have been at the surface. In fact, Japan Sea Bottom Water originates from coastal waters in the northern and northwestern reaches of the Sea of Japan. During some long-ago winter, this surface water became cold and dense enough to sink to the bottom of the sea.

When did this sinking occur?

Would it have been 10 or 100 years ago? Or maybe even 1000 years ago? If we define the year in which the water sank as year zero, and could somehow determine the elapsed time since that event (i.e., the age of the water mass), this would be nearly equivalent to the timescale of thermohaline circulation in the Sea of Japan.

As you might already have guessed, this is where radiocarbon (^{14}C) comes in. The age of Japan Sea Bottom Water can be revealed by ^{14}C, which is a kind of "stopwatch."

Today, seawater ^{14}C analysis is typically performed by using accelerator mass spectrometry. Because this method counts all of the ^{14}C atoms in a sample, it can be performed on just a few hundred milliliters of seawater. In the late 1970s however, this method had not yet been developed. The only way to perform ^{14}C analysis at the time was to patiently measure the weak beta radiation emitted by the small fraction of a sample's total ^{14}C that undergoes radiative decay during any given period. To obtain accurate measurements, this analysis has to be performed on the ^{14}C contained within a huge 200-L water sample.

At the Horibe lab, where I worked, we were steadily developing a

FIGURE 3-9: This large-scale water sampler was used to perform the first radiocarbon measurements in the Sea of Japan. It consists of two water samplers each with an internal volume of 250 L, and can collect water from two different depths.

massive water sampler capable of collecting 250-L samples from the deep ocean to obtain the necessary quantity of ^{14}C (fig. 3-9). Luckily for me, this water-sampling device was completed and first used in 1977 aboard the *Hakuho Maru* (at the time, I was in the second year of a doctoral program), and 200-L samples of Japan Sea Bottom Water were collected from each of the Sea of Japan's three major basins.

Each 200-L seawater sample was then transferred to a stainless steel drum, and the total inorganic carbon (ΣCO_2) was extracted on the spot. When carbon dioxide (CO_2) dissolves in seawater, it reacts with water molecules to form carbonic acid (H_2CO_3), a weak acid, which can further dissociate into bicarbonate (HCO_3^-) and carbonate (CO_3^{2-}) ions. The combination of all of these chemical species is referred to as "total inorganic carbon."

To extract total inorganic carbon, we first acidified each seawater sample by adding hydrochloric acid, which converts all of these chemical species into carbon dioxide. Then, we piped pure nitrogen gas into the stainless steel drums to flush the carbon dioxide out of solution. The now gaseous carbon dioxide was then absorbed in 1 L of concentrated alkaline solution and brought back to land for analysis of ^{14}C.

≋

3-13
We Established the Age of Japan Sea Bottom Water!

At the time, the University Storage Center for Research Materials on the University of Tokyo's Hongo Campus housed the C-14 Dating Laboratory, which was equipped with a high-performance ^{14}C analyzer and other instruments needed for ^{14}C measurement. To determine the age of a sample, acetylene gas (C_2H_2) was synthesized from the collected carbon, and the beta radiation emitted by the ^{14}C was measured over several days.

Time was of the essence. No matter what, I needed to finish these measurements by 1979, when my three-year doctoral program ended. It was do or die: from 1977 to 1978, I frequented the Hongo campus and devoted myself to the analysis of ^{14}C in Japan Sea Bottom Water.

However, I was also aware that marine ^{14}C analysis suffers from a serious problem. This is because seawater can contain ^{14}C from two different sources: one is natural ^{14}C, and the other originates in atmospheric nuclear tests conducted by the United States and the former Soviet Union in the 1960s.

This would not be a problem if the bottom water sank into the deep sea before the advent of atmospheric testing, but any water that sank during or after this period would be contaminated by artificial ^{14}C. The younger the bottom water, the stronger the effect of this contamination becomes. This error needed to be accounted for to accurately calculate the age of bottom-water samples.

I paid careful attention to the artificial ^{14}C problem while analyzing the ^{14}C data obtained from Japan Sea Bottom Water. In essence, what I did was to use a basic oceanographic model known as a box model to calculate how much seawater would have to have been exchanged between the surface and deep-water layers for the balance of total inorganic carbon and ^{14}C in each layer to match the observed data.

I won't delve into the details here (you can read about them in the paper I wrote at the time: Gamo and Horibe, 1983), but in the end I estimated that the bottom water was 200–400 years old. (Since then, after some slight changes to the model assumptions were suggested and implemented, this range has been revised somewhat downward to 100–200 years.)

The uncertainty in the age is because Japan Sea Bottom Water is much younger than the half-life of ^{14}C (5730 years), and this means that the decline in ^{14}C due to radiative decay is quite small. Nevertheless, there is no doubt that the timescale of thermohaline circulation in the Sea of Japan is on the order of a hundred years.

This is how it became apparent that the timescale of the Sea of Japan's thermohaline circulation is an order of magnitude smaller than the 1000–2000-year circulation of the oceans as a whole.

≈

3-14
Understanding Pathways of Bottom-Water Circulation: Two Measurements Converge

In section 1-5-2, I explained that the area offshore of Vladivostok in Russia's Primorsky Krai seems to be especially favorable for bottom-water formation (fig. 1-2).

Newly-formed bottom water can be distinguished by its extremely high oxygen concentration. As this bottom water moves throughout the Sea of Japan, its oxygen concentration gradually declines. One very useful way of understanding circulation patterns within the "bathtub" known as the Sea of Japan would be to measure the distribution of oxygen concentrations in bottom water.

However, this is very difficult to do in the current research environment. As I mentioned in column 2 at the end of chapter 2, the Sea of Japan is divided into the EEZs of several nations as established by the United Nations Convention of the Law of the Sea. The southeastern half of the Sea of Japan is contained within Japan's EEZ, and therefore can be freely accessed by Japanese researchers. However, the northwestern half is contained within the EEZs of other nations. In particular, the western part of the Japan Basin, where conditions are especially

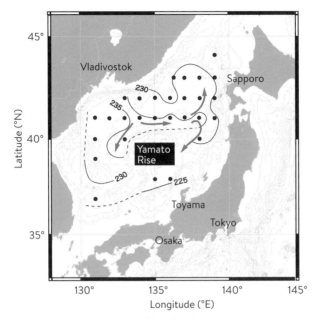

FIGURE 3-10: *Distribution of dissolved-oxygen concentrations (μmol/kg) in Japan Sea Bottom Water (i.e., at depths below 2000 m). The black contour lines indicate areas of constant oxygen concentration. Arrows indicate the direction of bottom-water flow as estimated from the oxygen data. The oxygen data were collected in 1969 by the Japan Meteorological Agency (1971).*

conducive to surface-water sinking, is mostly contained within Russia's EEZ. No matter how badly Japanese researchers may want to gain access to the Russian EEZ, obtaining permission for Japanese research ships to do so is extremely difficult.

Fortunately, in 1969, long before the creation of EEZs, the Japan Meteorological Agency carried out simultaneous observations across almost the entire Sea of Japan. The resulting dataset is a highly valuable resource for understanding the nature of Japan Sea Bottom Water. As expected, the highest value for dissolved oxygen (around 235 μmol/kg)

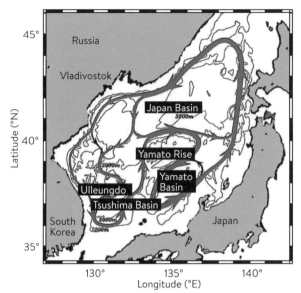

FIGURE 3–11:
Circulation patterns
of Japan Sea Bottom
Water as estimated
from current meter
measurements
(modified from
Senjyu et al., 2005).

occurs offshore of Vladivostok (fig. 3-10). Oxygen concentrations gradually decline with distance away from this point. By following the path of the oxygen decline, we can see that the bottom water generated offshore of Vladivostok appears to split into two branches upon encountering the Yamato Rise to its immediate south: one branch flows eastward, the other to the southwest.

The southwestward branch of bottom-water flow skirts the west face of the Yamato Rise, but flows without additional branching into the Tsushima Basin. The eastward branch skirts the north face of the Yamato Rise until it encounters the Japanese archipelago, at which point it splits into northward- and southward-flowing branches; the latter branch flows into the Yamato Basin.

This kind of bottom-water flow can also be measured directly by conducting long-term observations using a device known as a "current meter." In fact, as part of the CREAMS project, physical oceanographer Tomoharu Senjyu (Associate Professor, Kyushu University) installed numerous current meters near the seafloor in 1999–2000 to measure flow direction and strength across the Sea of Japan. The resulting data demonstrate that as the bottom water moves south from the vicinity of Vladivostok, it appears to circulate in a counterclockwise direction in the three basins: the Japan, Yamato, and Tsushima Basins (fig. 3-11).

The bottom-water circulation measured by using current meters (fig. 3-11) is largely consistent with that estimated based upon dissolved oxygen (fig. 3-10). Therefore, it seems apparent that the 100–200-year circulation of bottom water in the Sea of Japan follows the flow pattern shown in these figures. In this way, we are gradually gaining a clearer understanding of the deepest reaches of the Sea of Japan's "bathtub."

~~~~~~~~~~~~~~~~~~~~~~~~~~~~~ *Column 3* ~~~~~~~~~~~~~~~~~~~~~~~~~~~~~

How Temperature and Salinity Determine the Characteristics of Seawater

Throughout this book, I have used the terms "temperature" and "salinity" to describe the precise characteristics of seawater. However, when I use the term "temperature," I actually mean something slightly different than what probably springs to mind. Instead of the "local" (or *in situ*) temperature you might sense if you touched a water sample at depth, I am usually referring to what is known as "potential temperature."

Potential temperature is what you get when you subtract the influence of local water pressure from the locally measured temperature. When rigorous discussions are conducted about the ocean, and especially the deep ocean, potential temperature is generally preferred over locally measured temperature.

Why might this be? All regions of the ocean are subjected to increasing water pressure with depth. At the ocean's surface, the Earth's atmosphere exerts a pressure defined as one atmosphere (1 atm). Water pressure increases by 1 atm for every 10 m of depth, meaning that there is 100 atm of pressure at 1000 m and 500 atm at 5000 m. What is at issue is that increasing pressures also lead to slight increases in temperature. In technical terms, this is described as a rise in temperature due to adiabatic compression.

Water temperature is an important physical property that can be used to track a parcel of seawater through time. However, if the temperature of the seawater parcel were to deviate from its original value because of changes in depth (i.e., water pressure), this would make tracking water movements very difficult.

This is where the virtual temperature scale called "potential temperature" comes in. The potential temperature of a parcel of seawater is the temperature that the water would have if it were brought to the surface of the ocean (i.e., zero water pressure) without exchanging any heat with

~~~~~~

~~~~~~~~~~~~~~~~~~~~~~~ *Column 3* ~~~~~~~~~~~~~~~~~~~~~~~

its surroundings (i.e., adiabatically). In short, it describes the water temperature minus the effects of water pressure. Because potential temperature is a theoretical value, it cannot be measured directly. However, potential temperature can be calculated if *in situ* temperature, water pressure, and salinity are known.

The difference between *in situ* and potential temperatures becomes greater at higher water pressures. For example, let's look at how the locally measured temperature of a parcel of 10°C surface water with salinity 35 changes as it sinks into the deep sea without heat exchange with surrounding water. At a depth of 50 m, the *in situ* temperature, 10.06°C, is only slightly higher than when the water was at the surface. At 3000 m, however, the *in situ* temperature rises to 10.40°C, and at 5000 m, it reaches 10.73°C.

Despite the fact that we are talking about a single parcel of water, the actual *in situ* temperatures differ at each depth. If we look at potential temperature, in contrast, it remains 10.00°C at every depth, which makes it easier to track the water parcel over time.

Another basic property of seawater is its salinity. Salinity is defined as grams of salt per kilogram of seawater. In oceanography, we often use what is called the "practical salinity scale." In this scale, units are usually not appended to the salinity value. For example, a salinity of 34 means that 1 kg of seawater would contain 34 g of salt. (Previously, the sign "‰" [pronounced "per mille"] was often appended to salinity values, but this is no longer in use today.)

Incidentally, the word "salinity" necessarily implies a salt concentration. I sometimes see people use the phrase "salinity concentration," but this is incorrect, as it is equivalent to the nonsensical phrase "salt concentration concentration." If you simply must use the word "concentration," consider "salt concentration" instead.

The History of the Sea of Japan: How Did It First Emerge and How Has It Changed?

Long ago, the landmasses that would become the Japanese archipelago were contiguous with the Eurasian continent. Then, 20 million years ago, the Sea of Japan was born. Its subsequent history is now being reconstructed based upon careful examination of rock and sediment records.

With the arrival of the current ice age some 2.5 million years ago, the Earth entered a period of fluctuating temperatures. Global sea levels rose and fell by 100 m or more as the climate cycled between glacial and interglacial periods. The glacial periods brought low sea levels that further isolated the Sea of Japan from nearby seas and oceans. In turn, this isolation repeatedly triggered major environmental changes such as shutdowns of the thermohaline circulation and complete deoxygenation of the bottom water...

4-1
The Origin of the Sea of Japan: Our Story Begins 20 Million Years Ago

In chapters 1–3, I discussed the current state of the Sea of Japan in great detail. In this chapter, I will instead turn my focus to the past and travel back to the time when the Sea of Japan was born.

First and foremost, how long has the Sea of Japan existed in its current position in the western North Pacific? And how long is this history relative to the 4.5-billion-year history of Earth itself?

These are not questions that can be answered by history textbooks that go back a mere 500 years (i.e., to the Muromachi period) or 1000 years (i.e., to the Heian period in Japan or the Middle Ages in Europe). In fact, 1000 years ago, the Sea of Japan would have appeared more or less exactly as it does now. To reach the beginning of the Sea of Japan's geological history, you would need to travel some 10 or 20 million years back in time. Compared to this vast timescale, 1000 or 2000 years is only an instant, just a blink of an eye.

Over Earth's history, the continents have repeatedly split and merged back together into a single "supercontinent" in a cycle that plays out over several hundred million years. The most recent supercontinent is known as "Pangea" and is thought to have resulted from the merging of all of Earth's continents some 200 million years ago. Over time, this supercontinent broke apart, and its various pieces drifted into the arrangement that we are familiar with today.

The driving forces behind this continental motion are large-scale thermal convection currents that occur deep in the Earth's mantle and magmatism caused when parts of the mantle erupt from the crust. Our understanding of these forces forms part of what is known as the theory of plate tectonics. The origin of the Sea of Japan also falls under the purview of this theory.

Figure 4-1a shows the geography of the western North Pacific around 30 million years ago, during what is known in geology as the Oligocene Epoch of the Cenozoic Era. At this point, there was still no visible sign

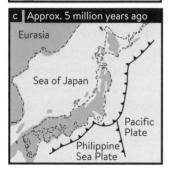

FIGURE 4–1: How the Sea of Japan and the Japanese archipelago were formed. Landmasses are indicated by dark grey shading, and oceans and seas by light grey shading. The black lines that appear somewhat like cold fronts on a meteorological chart show plate-to-plate boundaries where an oceanic plate is subducting (i.e., sinking) under a continental plate. The panels illustrate a probable timeline for the formation of the Sea of Japan and the separation of the Japanese archipelago from the Eurasian continent. (a) Until 30 million years ago, the Japanese archipelago was still part of the Eurasian continent. (b) By 16 million years ago, the Sea of Japan was expanding and pieces of land began to separate from the continent. (c) By 5 million years ago, the shape of the Japanese archipelago was similar to its shape today. (from https://www.gsj.jp/event/2008fy-event/akita2008/pos-index.html#index).

of the Japanese archipelago or the Sea of Japan. The land that made up the Japanese archipelago was then still part of the Eurasian continent. To put the geologic timescale into perspective, we are talking about a time period that came quite a long time after the extinction of the dinosaurs, which happened around 65 million years ago.

Around 20 million years ago, the eastern edge of the Eurasian continent developed a fissure that gradually began to expand. This was the beginning of the Sea of Japan. At this early stage, the newly emerging sea appeared somewhat like a small embayment. This sea—or rather, this fissure in the land—gradually widened and pushed the landmass that would eventually become the Japanese archipelago toward the southeast.

By measuring paleomagnetism (also known as residual magnetism) in the igneous rock in this region, it is possible to determine the direction the rock was facing in the geomagnetic field when it first formed from cooling magma or lava. By examining changes in these directions over the period during which the Sea of Japan was forming, researchers have deduced that the landmasses that correspond to present-day northeastern Japan rotated counterclockwise as they separated from the Eurasian continent, while the landmasses corresponding to present-day southwestern Japan rotated in the opposite direction (fig. 4-1b).

Viewed from the Pacific, it is as if the two halves of the Japanese archipelago were each one of a set of double doors that were being pulled outward away from the Eurasian continent. This motion created the curved shape that we see today.

The paleomagnetic record also tells us that the Sea of Japan continued to expand until around 14 million years ago. In other words, this is when the Sea of Japan and the Japanese archipelago first arrived at their current positions relative to the Eurasian continent. The 14 million years that have elapsed since this point represent only 0.3% of the 4.5 billion years of Earth's history; from a geologic perspective, it is an extremely recent event.

In the subsequent time period, the Japanese archipelago continued to gradually change shape due to shifting tectonic plates, colliding landmasses, and magmatic activity. However, the archipelago is thought to have basically reached its current shape some 5 million years ago (fig. 4-1c).

≈

4-2
Why Did the Sea of Japan Form When It Did?

Research on sediment layers and rock geology has almost conclusively established that the Sea of Japan first emerged around 20 million years ago and reached its current size around 14 million years ago. But why did the Sea of Japan grow to the size it did, and why did this growth happen during this period?

These questions are of great interest. Although something must have triggered these geological events, a specific mechanism has not yet been adequately described. We will have to await further research to obtain a definitive answer, but in the meantime, the following hypothesis is considered the most likely (fig. 4-2).

Plate tectonic theory tells us that a major incident with far-reaching consequences took place around 20 million years before the formation of the Sea of Japan: the Indian subcontinent, a vast landmass that had been drifting northward through the Indian Ocean, collided with the Eurasian continent. The huge compressive forces that resulted along the boundary between the two landmasses raised the Himalayan Mountains and the Tibetan Plateau. At the same time, the collision affected the underlying mantle and appears to have triggered new mantle currents that flowed eastward and westward from the Indian subcontinent.

The eastward mantle flow in particular is posited by many scholars to have caused deformations in the continental crust across East Asia and opened up numerous fissures that run along a northeast-to-southwest axis. In turn, these fissures may have increased magmatic activity in the region.

The expansion of one such fissure near the eastern margin of the Eurasian continent would have created the Sea of Japan, and a similar fissure to the south would have created the South China Sea at around the same time. Also, an example of continued magmatic activity stemming from a fissure in East Asia is the Okinawa Trough, an undersea volcanic belt on the northwestern side of the Ryukyu Islands.

Incidentally, the collision of the Indian subcontinent with Eurasia,

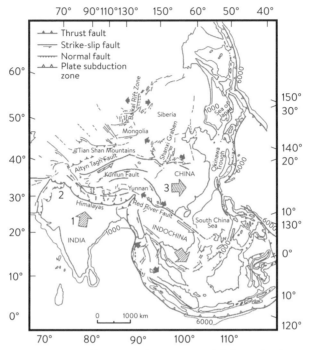

FIGURE 4–2: *An illustration showing crustal deformation in East Asia caused by collision with the Indian subcontinent. The Indian subcontinent (1) collided with the Eurasian continent, (2) uplifting the Himalayas and the Tibetan Plateau and (3) creating an eastward flow in the underlying mantle (based on Taira, 1990).*

and the subsequent uplift of the Tibetan Plateau, had another important effect: it established a new atmospheric circulation system over Asia. In fact, it stimulated the development of the cold wintertime Siberian air mass that is responsible for the strong and cold winter monsoon winds that blow across the Sea of Japan.

In other words, the collision of the Indian subcontinent with Asia had profound and far-reaching effects including the creation of the Sea of

Japan and the simultaneous strengthening of northwesterly monsoon winds. These two factors combined would eventually bring large snow-fall totals to the Japanese archipelago. You could compare these complex interconnected events to a long cascade of falling dominoes over a period of tens of millions of years across the vastness of the whole of East Asia.

≋

4-3
What If the Sea of Japan Were Larger?

What follows is purely a thought experiment from my imagination. What if the Sea of Japan had not stopped expanding 14 million years ago? What would have happened if it had continued to expand up to the present day?

In this scenario, tectonic forces would have shifted the Japanese archipelago farther east, pushing it farther away from the Eurasian con-tinent and leaving it stranded in the middle of the ocean. Clearly, this would make it more difficult to reach Japan from the continent. In the real world, modern humans are thought to have reached the Japanese archipelago around 30,000–40,000 years ago. In this alternate scenario, however, their arrival would undoubtedly have been delayed.

Let's consider some other thought experiments. What if the expan-sion of the Sea of Japan (which occurred from 14–20 million years ago) had been delayed to such an extent that the Japanese archipelago was currently still contiguous with the Eurasian continent? Or what if the expansion of the Sea of Japan ended much sooner, and the Japanese archipelago was substantially closer to the continent than it is today?

In both of these scenarios, we can be confident that Japan's climate would more closely resemble a cold and dry continental climate. Would Japan's unique civilization, which has been nurtured over the years by a warm and humid environment, have emerged in this alternate world? Or, in this scenario of desolate weather and increased threat from neigh-boring countries, would the nation of Japan even exist? I hesitate to answer either of these questions with a "yes."

Yet the real world did not unfold along any of these alternate scenarios. In reality, modern humans emerged in Africa, migrated across the Eurasian continent, and reached the Japanese archipelago some 30,000–40,000 years ago. When they did so, the version of the Sea of Japan that they crossed was already precisely the right size. Truth is indeed stranger than fiction. Don't you agree?

≈

4-4
Lurching between Recurring Glacial and Interglacial Periods

That's enough speculation. Let's return to our original story and trace the history of the Sea of Japan after its initial emergence.

Around 2.58 million years ago, at the start of the Quaternary period in the Cenozoic era, the Earth's climate entered a period of cooling. This was the beginning of what is known as an "ice age." In an ice age, relatively cold "glacial periods" are typically followed by relatively warm "interglacial periods" in a cycle that repeats around every 100,000 years. The temperature difference between glacial and interglacial periods varies by region and time period, but generally tends to be around 5–10°C. The Sea of Japan, which by this time was very similar in shape to how it is today, was severely impacted by these climate fluctuations.

The Sea of Japan is particularly sensitive to changes in sea level (the height of the ocean's surface). Global sea level fluctuates by about 100 m between glacial and interglacial periods. During cold glacial periods, much of the rain that falls over land freezes into glaciers instead of flowing through rivers back to the sea. The outcome is a net transfer of water from oceans to land, which lowers global sea levels.

Over the past 800,000 years, sea level has clearly risen and fallen periodically (fig. 4-3). To understand how sea level might have affected past environmental conditions in the Sea of Japan, researchers have turned

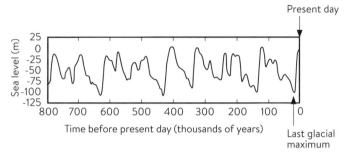

FIGURE 4–3: *A reconstruction of sea-level fluctuations over the past 800,000 years. Historical sea levels are shown relative to current mean sea level (modified from Bintanja et al., 2005).*

to seafloor sediments. Seafloor sediments are created by the gradual settling of small particles (for example, organic matter from marine organisms [i.e., marine snow] and wind-borne dust) that sink through the water column. Newer sediment deposits accumulate on top of older deposits such that each layer of sediment corresponds to a specific time. By analyzing the chemical characteristics of sediment layers and examining embedded fossils, researchers can learn about changes in the chemistry of the seawater and seabed over time.

On land, for example, you have probably noticed layers in the soil where the side of a mountain has been cut away to make space for a road. Often, these layers are folded in a way that resembles undulating waves. You may even have spent some time digging through such soil to collect fossils of marine organisms. This is possible because in some regions, these soil layers once existed as seafloor sediment deposits before they were uplifted onto land.

Researchers collect seafloor sediments by pushing a sturdy pipe into the seabed. What secrets about the past are buried in sediments in the Sea of Japan?

≋

FIGURE 4–4:
*The scientific
drilling ship* JOIDES
Resolution. *The
huge derrick in the
center of the ship
is used to lower
the drill string
to the seafloor.
Photographed by the
author in 1990.*

4-5
The Sea of Japan's Seafloor Sediments Contain a Record of Its Glacial Environment: Evidence of a "Dead Zone"

In 1989, the scientific drilling ship *JOIDES Resolution* (fig. 4-4), the main research ship of the Ocean Drilling Program (ODP), collected seafloor sediments from the Sea of Japan (ODP Leg 127). It drilled boreholes at four sampling locations across the Japan and Yamato Basins and collected cylindrical sediment samples, known as "sediment cores," that were each several hundred meters in length.

These four sediment cores share some very interesting similarities. Figure 4-5 (plate 6) shows a longitudinal section of a sediment core (this is known as a "half-core photo") obtained by cutting the core lengthwise into two equal pieces. In these sections, you can see that there is a repeating pattern of black and white layers as you go from the top of the core to the bottom—that is, from the present to the past. This pattern stretches across 2.5 million years' worth of sediment layers, starting from when glacial–interglacial cycles first began and continuing uninterrupted to the present day.

The black layers are rich in organic matter, but the white layers contain almost none. What does this odd repeating pattern tell us? Seafloor sedi-

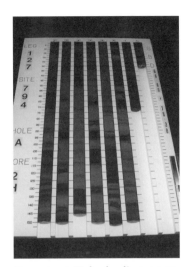

Figure 4–5: Halved sediment core collected from the Sea of Japan in 1989 by the Ocean Drilling Program (photograph courtesy of Ryuji Tada).

ments in the Sea of Japan are strongly influenced by Japan Sea Bottom Water, which is in direct contact with the seabed. Changes in the properties of Japan Sea Bottom Water are reflected in the composition of seafloor sediments.

When Japan Sea Bottom Water contains very little oxygen and is highly reducing, sinking organic matter will reach the seafloor without being completely decomposed. This incompletely decomposed organic matter covers the seabed in the form of a sludge that then gets buried under the next layer of sediments. Sediment deposits formed in this way are characterized by their dark coloration.

On the other hand, when Japan Sea Bottom Water contains abundant oxygen and is highly oxidizing, sinking organic matter can undergo complete aerobic decomposition. Sediment deposits formed in this way are characterized by their light coloration, which is primarily the color of inorganic sediments. In some cases, these sediments contain many so-called "trace fossils," which are formed when benthic organisms dig into the seabed.

In other words, the striped pattern in figure 4-5 shows that Japan Sea Bottom Water has frequently switched between oxygen-rich and oxygen-poor states over the past 2.5 million years. Once the various layers of the sediment core have been dated, it becomes clear that sections of the sediment with many black layers correspond to past glacial periods, whereas sections with many white layers correspond to interglacial periods. This means that during glacial periods, the deep water in the Sea of Japan was often nearly or completely anoxic.

As I have explained in earlier chapters, surface-water downwelling is the only mechanism that can supply oxygen to the bottom water of the Sea of Japan. During glacial periods, the lower sea level meant that the sea floor was in fact closer to the surface than during interglacial periods. Yet surface-water downwelling was much less active during this time. To put it another way, the conditions did not favor the creation of sufficiently dense surface water to drive thermohaline circulation.

Consider the example of the Black Sea, which I introduced in the column at the end of chapter 1. In this "dead zone," oxygen concentrations fall to zero below a depth of 150 m. As a consequence, oxygen-breathing organisms cannot survive at depth. At one time, these same things were true of the Sea of Japan.

What could have caused this to happen?

≋

4-6
A World Where Sea Levels Were 120 Meters Lower

I mentioned in section 4-4 that sea levels fall during glacial periods because some ocean water becomes trapped on land in the form of terrestrial ice. During the last glacial maximum (the most recent time when glaciers were at their greatest extent; see fig. 4-3), which occurred about 20,000 years ago, terrestrial glaciation was especially widespread, and global sea levels are estimated to have fallen to about 120 m below the current level.

It goes without saying that this global sea-level decline also applies to the Sea of Japan. As sea levels fall, parts of the seabed increasingly emerge above water and become part of the land. Figure 4-6 shows a reconstruction of the Sea of Japan's coastline during the last glacial maximum.

As you can see, nearly the whole of the Seto Inland Sea was above water. Similarly, the Strait of Tartary, which is only about 10-m deep, and the La Pérouse Strait, which is about 50-m deep, would have also been completely above water. By contrast, the Tsushima and Tsugaru Straits, which are about 130-m deep at their deepest points, would have been

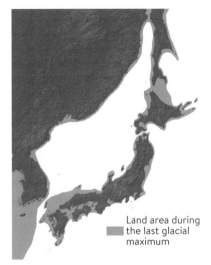

FIGURE 4-6: Estimated location of the coastline along the Sea of Japan during the last glacial maximum (approx. 20,000 years ago; figure downloaded from http://www.osaka-kyoiku.ac.jp/~syamada/map_syamada/PhysicalGeography/C111220Map_Japan_LGM_PhysGeogII2011b.jpg).

Land area during the last glacial maximum

0   250 500   1000km

right on the dividing line between land and sea.

Were the Tsushima and Tsugaru Straits dry or filled with water at this time? This question has attracted the interest of numerous researchers who have at times held differing opinions.

The Tsushima Strait is likely to have just barely persisted as a seawater corridor. Based on its current bathymetry, the strait would have been about 10-20-m deep and 15-km wide during the last glacial maximum. Also, the discovery of fossilized shellfish that date to this time indicate that the strait was probably inundated with seawater.

This does not mean, however, that the strait would have functioned as it does today. In fact, it is estimated that the flow rate of the Tsushima Warm Current through the strait would have been less than 1% of current levels.

As with the Tsushima Strait, the Tsugaru Strait seems to have persisted as a seawater channel with a depth of about 10-20 m. However, it would have only been about 2-3-km wide, making it even narrower than the Tsushima Strait.

≈

4-7
What Triggered the Shift from a "Dead Zone" to a "Sea of Life"?

As with the Seto Inland Sea, the East China Sea was also mostly above water during the last glacial maximum. In effect, the shoreline on the continental side had advanced to a point just west of the Japanese archipelago. As a result, large amounts of low-salinity coastal water that had been heavily influenced by the Yangtze and other river outflows ended up near the entrance to the Tsushima Strait.

One constant between both glacial and interglacial periods is that the Sea of Japan always receives fresh-water input from rivers, which tends to decrease salinity. During the last glacial maximum, it is estimated that the almost complete absence of high-salinity input from the Tsushima Warm Current allowed the surface salinity of the Sea of Japan to decline to about two-thirds of what it is today. This would have caused a corresponding decline in surface-water density and weight.

In turn, this would have stabilized and strengthened the stratified structure of the water column (an arrangement in which light surface water floats atop heavy deep water; see section 2-1) to such an extent that no amount of surface-water cooling could overturn it. Under these conditions, thermohaline circulation is likely to have essentially stopped.

Without thermohaline circulation, there is no way to supply oxygen to the deep and bottom waters of the Sea of Japan. As I explained in section 2-3, oxygen gas is only produced in the photosynthetically active surface waters. This abundance of oxygen supports a high biomass in the surface ocean, which in turn exports substantial amounts of organic matter (e.g., marine snow) into the deep ocean.

In the deep ocean, the decomposition of this sinking organic matter consumes available oxygen. In the absence of some mechanism to deliver oxygen from the surface ocean, dissolved-oxygen concentrations fall to zero as the deep water becomes anoxic. This is the mechanism that leads to a "dead zone," and is in fact the same mechanism I discussed in my column on the Black Sea at the end of chapter 1.

In the case of the Sea of Japan, scientists have estimated that it would take only 200–300 years for the bottom water to become anoxic following a shutdown of the thermohaline circulation. This estimate is based upon observed declines in bottom-water oxygen concentrations that are currently occurring in the Sea of Japan due to human-caused global environmental change (I will cover this topic in detail in chapter 6).

Once a glacial period comes to an end and an interglacial period begins, glaciers retreat and sea levels begin to rise. Even during glacial periods, sea levels may rise temporarily during brief intervals of warming. In either scenario, the Tsugaru and Tsushima Straits will become deeper and wider, which would increase the flow of seawater into the Sea of Japan from its surrounding seas and oceans. This increased inflow will have the effect of increasing surface-water salinity, which will in turn facilitate the formation of heavy surface water that can sink into the deep sea. Once this downwelling water reaches the bottom-water layer, oxygen levels in this layer will begin to increase.

Throughout the ice age, the environment of Japan Sea Bottom Water has shifted from oxidizing (i.e., oxygen is present and aerobic organisms can survive), to reducing (i.e., oxygen is absent and aerobic organisms cannot survive), and then back to oxidizing again, and so on. These frequent fluctuations from one state to the other account for the black and white striping of seafloor sediment cores that I described earlier (see fig. 4-5).

In chapter 2, I mentioned that the Sea of Japan is extremely sensitive to environmental change. This is true not only of the present but also of the past. In fact, as can be seen in its frequent and drastic environmental fluctuations, the Sea of Japan has functioned as a "canary of the oceans" throughout its history.

≈

4-8
The Sea of Japan's History Is Recorded in the Organisms That Lived Through It

Scientists have used many different kinds of fossils to reconstruct the paleoenvironments (i.e., past environments) of the Sea of Japan. When I say "fossils," however, I am referring not to the large fossils you might imagine but to fossilized organisms that are so small they can be identified only under a microscope.

Some of the most useful of these organisms are small protozoans known as "foraminifera." These microscopic organisms are distinguished by their calcium carbonate shells, which are known as "tests." You might be familiar with "star sand," which is often sold in souvenir shops in Okinawa and the Yaeyama Islands southwest of Japan. Although it resembles a fine-grained sand with star-like protrusions, star sand is actually composed of the tests of a particular species of foraminifera that lives on tropical coral reefs.

Foraminifera can be divided into two main groups: "benthic" foraminifera inhabit the seafloor and "planktonic" foraminifera float freely in the water column. Both groups can be found in fossil form in seafloor sediments. Once these fossils have been carefully extracted, scientists examine species prevalence (i.e., community composition), test morphology, chemical composition, isotope ratio, etc., to determine where the samples lived and what water temperatures they experienced when they were alive. Benthic foraminifera provide information on past conditions in the bottom water. Planktonic foraminifera, on the other hand, provide information on surface waters.

For example, some planktonic foraminifera have tests that grow in a spiral, much like a conch shell. Studies have shown that the spirals grow in different orientations depending on whether the temperature exceeds a certain threshold. At temperatures above the threshold, the tests grow in right-handed spirals, but below the threshold, they form left-handed spirals. By examining the ratio of right- to left-handed spirals in a sample of tests from a particular time period, researchers can determine whether water temperature at the time was high or low. You might be wondering why water temperature affects tests in this way. Frustratingly, scientists do not currently have a good answer to this question.

Other types of information can be obtained by chemical analysis. For example, the oxygen isotope ratios in the calcium carbonate ($CaCO_3$) in foraminiferal tests are good indicators of water temperature when the foraminifera were alive. Specifically, scientists measure the ratio of oxygen with an atomic mass of 18 (^{18}O) to oxygen with an atomic mass of 16 (^{16}O) (normally, this ratio is around 1:500). Lab experiments have shown that foraminiferal tests have lower $^{18}O/^{16}O$ ratios when grown at high temperatures. In fact, each 1°C increase in water temperature translates to a roughly 0.02% decline in $^{18}O/^{16}O$. Therefore, by measuring $^{18}O/^{16}O$ ratios in fossil foraminifera collected from seafloor sediments, scientists can reconstruct the water temperature experienced by these organisms when they were alive (i.e., the paleotemperature). However, one important drawback to this method is that the $^{18}O/^{16}O$ ratio of fossil foraminifera is affected not only by water temperature but also by the $^{18}O/^{16}O$ ratio of seawater (primarily in the form of H_2O).

Fortunately, there is a second way to estimate past water temperatures. Calcium carbonate tests also contain about 0.1–1% magnesium carbonate ($MgCO_3$) as an impurity. The relative amount of magnesium (i.e., the Mg/Ca ratio) is known to increase with temperature. Therefore, the Mg/Ca ratio of fossil foraminifera can also be used to reconstruct paleotemperature records.

Another useful group of organisms is the diatoms. These are a type of silicon-containing phytoplankton that are also commonly found in fossil form in marine sediments. As with foraminifera, different diatom species have different habitat preferences. Therefore, by carefully examining their fossils, scientists can glean a variety of information about the past including where the diatoms came from and the paths of the ocean currents that carried them.

≈

4-9
What Do Fossils Tell Us?

Here is an example that explains how these techniques have been used. Figure 4-7 shows an overview of environmental changes that have occurred in the Sea of Japan over the past 95,000 years. This particular reconstruction was created by paleo-oceanographer Tadamichi Oba (Professor Emeritus, Hokkaido University) and his collaborators.

In chapter 3, I described the research cruises conducted in the Sea of Japan by the *Hakuho Maru* in 1977 and 1979. Although I mainly focused on seawater samples in that chapter, scientists on these cruises also collected several seafloor sediment cores. In fact, figure 4-7 is partly based on a 10-m long core, representing some 100,000 years of sedimentation, that Oba obtained from the Oki Ridge during one of these cruises. Together with his collaborators, Oba poured an extraordinary amount of effort into testing the sediment core and analyzing the available data. The information that was learned from this core led to important insights into the paleoenvironment of the Sea of Japan.

Let's go through the panels of figure 4-7 in chronological order. From 95,000 to 33,000 years ago, the climate progressively cooled. This inhibited surface-water downwelling and weakened the thermohaline circulation. Then, from 33,000 to 19,000 years ago, around the time of the last glacial maximum, the thermohaline circulation came to a complete stop. We know this because the sediment layers that correspond to this time period are devoid of benthic foraminifera. In the absence of oxygen input from the surface waters, the bottom waters had become anoxic, killing off benthic foraminifera and transforming the seabed into a landscape of death.

During the transition from a glacial to an interglacial climate some 19,000 to 10,000 years ago, the cold Oyashio Current began to flow through the Tsugaru Strait into the Sea of Japan. This is apparent in the species of benthic foraminifera that appear in the seafloor sediments of the time. Many are specific to the cold and shallow waters of the North Pacific, indicating that they were carried in on the Oyashio Current.

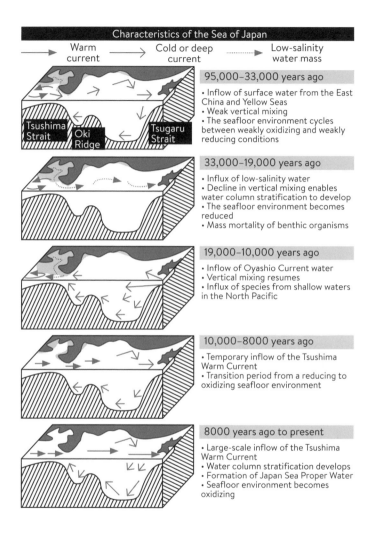

FIGURE 4-7: Reconstruction showing a timeline of environmental change in the Sea of Japan during and after the last glacial period. Light gray shading indicates the location of the coastline during the time period described in the figure (modified from Oba, 1983 based upon later research results [Oba, personal communication]).

With rising sea levels, the flow of the Tsushima Warm Current into the Sea of Japan gradually began to increase. This influx became especially noticeable about 8000 years ago. This can be seen from the rapid increase in abundance of fossilized planktonic foraminifera that are specific to the warm waters of the Kuroshio Current System, including those with right-hand coiling tests that I described above.

As you can see, these small organisms are eloquent chroniclers of the Sea of Japan's history. The traces they left behind in the sediment have much to tell us about the distant past.

≈

4-10
Fluctuations in the Tsushima Warm Current

How has the water temperature of the Sea of Japan changed over time?

Paleotemperature records estimated from oxygen isotope ratios ($^{18}O/^{16}O$) of planktonic foraminifera tests show that surface-water temperatures in the southern Sea of Japan were less than 10°C during glacial periods, but rose to nearly 20°C with the inflow of the Tsushima Warm Current.

In addition, the paleo-oceanographer Itaru Koizumi (Professor Emeritus, Hokkaido University) has provided important insights based upon the careful study of fossilized diatoms. His results, which show a rapid increase in diatom species that prefer warm environments, are consistent with the finding that large amounts of Tsushima Warm Current water began to flow into the Sea of Japan around 8000 years ago.

Incidentally, scientists have noticed an interesting quirk in the abundance of fossilized warm-current diatoms. Instead of staying constant from 8000 years ago to the present day, their abundance seems to have risen and fallen repeatedly. What could have caused these fluctuations?

The behavior of the Tsushima Warm Current is thought to be a key factor. In other words, the stronger the Tsushima Warm Current, the more diatoms from warm current systems settle in the Sea of Japan. As shown

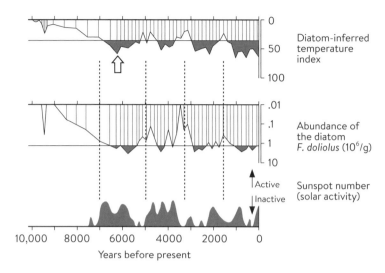

FIGURE 4–8: Relationship between periodic fluctuations in sunspot activity and strength of the Tsushima Warm Current (Koizumi, 1995). The panels show (from top to bottom) diatom-inferred temperature index ([abundance of warm-water species]/[total abundance of warm-water and cold-water species] × 100) based on fossil diatoms collected from bottom sediments on the Oki Ridge; changes in abundance of a single warm-water species (Fragilariopsis doliolus); and fluctuations in sunspot activity (from Eddy, 1981). Certain parts of the graphs were shaded gray to emphasize the peaks (Koizumi, 1995). The vertical dashed lines indicate a correlation between the diatom-inferred temperature index (fluctuation of the Tsushima Warm Current) and sunspot activity.

by the diatom-inferred temperature record, the Tsushima Warm Current peaked around 6300 years ago (indicated by the white arrow in fig. 4-8). Since then, the inflow of the Tsushima Warm Current seems to have followed an 1800-year cycle of repeated weakening and strengthening.

Why would the strength of the Tsushima Warm Current fluctuate in this way?

Koizumi noticed that periodic cycles in sunspot activity (increases or decreases in the number of sunspots) correlate with the strengthening and weakening of the Tsushima Warm Current as shown by vertical dashed lines in fig. 4-8. Sunspot activity affects the Earth's energy balance, which in turn can profoundly affect the global climate and environmental conditions. It seems likely that there is some mechanism by which sunspot activity creates fluctuations in the Tsushima Warm Current. This is an exciting research area, and I eagerly await future developments.

4-11
The Tsushima Warm Current Determines the Fate of the Sea of Japan

When the last glacial period came to an end and the global climate transitioned into an interglacial period, the "floodgate" of the Tsushima Strait opened once again and allowed the flow of the Tsushima Warm Current into the Sea of Japan to increase. This shift transformed the bottom layer of the Sea of Japan from a "dead zone" to one that overflowed with life.

The influx of warm water from the south also warmed the climate along the Sea of Japan coast. This increased evaporation from the surface ocean and stimulated the "natural desalination device" (see section 1-5-1) that is responsible for huge wintertime snowfall totals on the Japanese archipelago. With the return of a warm and humid environment, forests spread across the land.

From the perspective of the people of the Jomon period (a historical period that began about 16,000 years ago), these developments would have facilitated the gradual buildup of the abundant food resources that would allow their hunter-gatherer communities to flourish. Eventually, with the advent of rice farming, the people of the Japanese archipelago were able to secure a more reliable food supply. Even here, however, this shift to agriculture was made substantially easier by the archipelago's warm climate and plentiful water, which are well-suited to rice cultivation.

The influx of the Tsushima Warm Current also brought the relatively saline water of the Kuroshio Current System into the Sea of Japan. This raised the salinity of the surface water, thereby making it easier for this water to gain enough density in winter to sink into the deep sea. In turn, this increase in surface-water downwelling revived the thermohaline circulation, which had stalled when the deep water of the Sea of Japan was a "dead zone," and allowed the Sea of Japan's unique low-temperature, high-oxygen water mass—i.e., Japan Sea Proper Water—to spread throughout the deep- and bottom-water layers. This is how researchers believe Japan Sea Proper Water was created, and how it has persisted from the end of the last glacial period until the present day.

The resumption of a thermohaline circulation not only increased vertical mixing in the Sea of Japan through surface-water downwelling but also increased nutrient cycling between the surface and deep waters. The term "nutrient" encompasses a variety of chemical constituents that are required for phytoplankton photosynthesis, including nitrogen, phosphorous, and silicon. Recently, trace amounts of heavy metals such as iron, zinc, and nickel have also been found to be essential for phytoplankton. As such, they too are considered to be nutrients.

In the surface ocean, nutrients are absorbed by phytoplankton and used for growth. These phytoplankton are consumed by zooplankton, which in turn are consumed by small fishes, and so on. In this way, nutrients are passed through the food web and distributed throughout surface ocean organisms.

Some of the waste products and other organic material produced in the surface ocean are quickly decomposed back into their constituent nutrients and reabsorbed by phytoplankton. However, the remainder sinks into the deep sea. This is the source of marine snow, which I described near the end of section 2-3.

The organic matter that sinks as marine snow is broken down into its constituent nutrients by gradual aerobic decomposition. Figure 4-9 shows a simplified schematic of nutrient cycling in the surface and deep layers.

≋

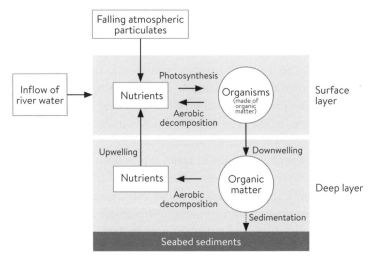

FIGURE 4–9: Nutrient cycling in the surface and deep ocean.

4-12
So Much Depends on the "Water of Life"

Thanks to the constant influx and decomposition of marine snow, Japan Sea Proper Water is rich in nutrients. Vertical mixing associated with thermohaline circulation helps bring this nutrient-rich water to the surface, thereby fertilizing the surface waters and boosting fisheries resources in the Sea of Japan.

The Tsushima Warm Current contributes to this process by bringing high-salinity surface waters into the Sea of Japan, but it is also important in another way: it not only contains water from the Kuroshio Current (which flows northward along the west coast of the island of Kyushu), but also contains water from the Taiwan Warm Current (which flows into the Tsushima Strait from the East China Sea). The Taiwan Warm Current incorporates fresh river water (chiefly from the Yangtze) along with abundant nutrients gleaned from continental-shelf sediment in the East China Sea. The salinity of the Taiwan Warm Current is lowered by river water outflow, the volume of which depends on climatic conditions on the continent (whether there is more or less rainfall).

Because the Taiwan Warm Current is less saline than the Kuroshio Current, it acts to lower the surface salinity of the Sea of Japan and inhibit thermohaline circulation. At the same time, its high nutrient levels help boost productivity in surface waters and increase the export of organic matter to the deep sea. The combination of these two effects may accelerate oxygen depletion at depth.

The environment of the Sea of Japan is in a state of delicate balance. In the future, factors such as the strength and water chemistry of the Tsushima Warm Current will continue to impact conditions in one way or another. Continuous and detailed observations of the physics and chemistry of the Tsushima Warm Current and the Sea of Japan are likely to reveal numerous links between the two.

~~~~~~~~~~~~~~~~~~ *Column 4* ~~~~~~~~~~~~~~~~~~

Seafloor Resources in the Sea of Japan: Methane Gas and Gas Hydrates

Methane gas hydrates are increasingly attracting attention as one of the Sea of Japan's unexploited natural resources.

Gas hydrates are gas molecules that are completely contained within a cage-like crystal structure composed of water (H_2O) molecules. To the naked eye, they have the appearance of a sherbet-like solid. The volume of gas that can be contained in this hydrate form far exceeds the solubility of gas in ordinary liquid water.

For example, methane (CH_4) is the main component of natural gas. Normally, its solubility in water is around 1–2 mol/L, depending on factors such as temperature. Compare this to the 10 mol/L of methane that can be contained in water in hydrate form. In other words, methane hydrates have the potential to become a high-yield resource of fossil fuels.

One problem, however, is that the hydrate structure is only stable under certain low-temperature and high-pressure conditions. For a gas hydrate to be stable at an ambient pressure of 1 atm, for example, the temperature must be at or below –15°C. This temperature constraint is relaxed under conditions of high water pressure. At a depth of 260 m (i.e., 26 atm), the temperature only has to be below 0°C, and at 760 m (i.e., 76 atm), it only has to be below 10°C. Because of these requirements, methane hydrates are naturally found only in permafrost and in deep seabeds.

Although methane hydrate looks like white ice when collected from the seafloor, it burns easily when lit, earning it the nickname "flammable ice." Japan's exclusive economic zone (EEZ; see the column at the end of chapter 2) is known to contain numerous methane hydrate deposits. The largest deposits are thought to be offshore of Japan's Pacific coast in the Nankai Trough, which is located off of the Kii Peninsula and the island of Shikoku. However, large deposits are also thought to exist in the Sea of

Japan, specifically offshore of the Joetsu region near Sado Island, near Okushiri Island, and near the Oki Islands. In fact, the very first methane hydrate sample collected in the waters around Japan was obtained in the Sea of Japan during the ODP's scientific drilling expedition in 1989, which I discussed in section 4-5.

By the way, why is there methane gas in seabed sediments in the first place? Methane is produced in sediments when microbes decompose organic matter in the absence of oxygen (i.e., in a reducing environment). In deeper, high-temperature sediments, some methane can also be produced from organic matter by thermal decomposition. Both of these sources of seafloor methane generation are known to occur in the Sea of Japan.

Currently, under the direction of the Ministry of Economy, Trade and Industry, researchers are studying new methods to accurately estimate methane hydrate reserves and mine methane hydrates from the Sea of Japan. The intention is to one day establish seafloor methane hydrates as an important energy resource. While we have high expectations for these efforts, we also must consider the urgent global challenge of decreasing the consumption of fossil fuels.

The Sea of Japan Is a "Mother Sea": Without It, Japan Would Not Exist

The end of the last glacial period heralds the beginning of a warm and humid climate across the Japanese archipelago. The Tsushima Warm Current starts to flow through the Tsushima Strait once more and a "natural desalination system" begins to operate in the Sea of Japan.

These changes provide a range of benefits to the residents of the Japanese archipelago just as the first green shoots of Japanese culture begin to sprout during the Jomon period. Eventually, active trading routes are established with countries around the Sea of Japan, spurring cultural advances across the region, and in the early-modern period, the flourishing of the kitamae shipping route becomes a major factor in promoting Japanese trade and culture.

The "Mother Sea" nurtured the nation of Japan into what it is today.

5-1
The Sea of Japan as It Was First Seen by Humans:
A Dialogue between a Student and an Elderly Professor

Here is a conversation between a student (A) and an elderly professor (B) that will review some of the key points of the previous chapter and introduce the subject of the current one.

A: Professor, when did humans first arrive in the Japanese archipelago?

B: I've wanted to know that myself! Sadly, there isn't a good answer to that yet. To work out what we know, let's start with the creation of the Japanese archipelago and move forward in time from there. When the Sea of Japan first reached its current size about 14 million years ago, humans did not yet exist. You might know this already. This was still millions of years before early humans such as Australopithecines and *Homo erectus* arrived on the scene. Currently, the oldest known hominin species is *Sahelanthropus tchadensis*, which was discovered in central Africa in 2001 and is thought to have lived around 7 million years ago.

A: Have any similar fossils been unearthed near Japan?

B: As far as fossils that were discovered in Asia, the best known are Java Man (0.7–1.2 million years ago) and Peking Man (200,000–700,000 years ago). Both belong to the species *Homo erectus*. Sadly, no human fossils of this age have been unearthed on the Japanese archipelago itself. The oldest human fossil discovered in Japan is the Yamashita Cave Man, which was unearthed in Okinawa; because the fossil dates back to about 32,000 years ago, it's probably an anatomically modern human (i.e., species *Homo sapiens*). One problem with searching for human fossils in the Japanese archipelago is that the acidic soil tends to degrade any buried bones. So it's possible that humans settled in the archipelago at an earlier time, but at the moment there is little evidence to suggest that they did.

A: Tell me more about modern humans. I read in a book that scientists have recently developed new methods of analysis based on fossil DNA . . .

FIGURE 5–1: The emergence of anatomically modern humans (Homo sapiens) and their dispersal routes to various regions around the world (figure modified from one produced by the National Museum of Nature and Science, Tokyo, 2001).

B: That's right. I can tell you've been studying. The term "anatomically modern human" refers to lineages that are our direct ancestors, meaning that we share most of the same genes. They are said to have emerged in Africa some 150,000–200,000 years ago. But did you know that there were also different human species that appeared at similar times?

A: Um, did they include the Neanderthals and Denisovans?

B: Yes! Although you don't sound very confident about your answer, considering how much you've been studying (laughs). Recent research suggests that modern humans carry some Neanderthal genes and that humans and Neanderthals interbred to some extent. Once the Neanderthals went extinct around 35,000 years ago, anatomically modern humans, as the only remaining human species, spread around the world.

A: How did modern humans migrate out of Africa and spread around the world?

B: Humans seem to have traveled through several routes to Europe, the Middle East, and Asia (fig. 5-1). Early on, humans would have been unable to cross large bodies of water. When they reached the ocean, they would have either settled along the coast or changed direction to continue moving over land. But it's important to remember that this happened ten thousand to several tens of thousands of years ago, during or immediately after the last glacial period, when Earth's ice sheets were quite large. As a result, sea levels are thought to have been 50–120 m lower than they are today. This means that, unlike today, there would have been a land bridge across the Bering Strait, and so people could walk directly from Eurasia to North America.

A: I'm confused about how long it took humans to reach New Zealand. Isn't it right next to Australia? But even though the first humans arrived in Australia 40,000 years ago, they didn't reach New Zealand until 1000 years ago, and when they did, it looks like it was through an extremely indirect route.

B: That's a great question. When humans first migrated from Southeast Asia to the Australian continent, much of the route was either over land or involved shallow straits that were narrow enough to see across and to navigate in early raft-like vessels. However, to get from Australia to New Zealand required crossing the formidable barrier of the Tasman Sea. The Tasman Sea is over 5000 m deep at its deepest point and over 2000 km wide from east to west. Even worse, weather conditions in the sea are often very challenging, with frequent strong winds. The seagoing technology of the time probably wasn't a match for these kinds of conditions. At first glance, Japan appears similar to New Zealand in that it is also an island nation. But in reality, the Japanese archipelago is much closer to the continent, and was therefore quite easy to access. Anatomically modern humans are thought to have reached the Japanese archipelago some 30,000–40,000 years ago.

A: So they crossed the Tsushima Strait in search of an undiscovered paradise?

B: Well, it's possible that they might have traveled across the East China Sea or a different part of the Sea of Japan instead, but based on ease of access, I think it's most likely that they would have chosen to cross the Tsushima Strait. They would have done so during the last glacial period, meaning that sea levels were lower and the Tsushima Strait was much narrower and shallower than it is today. They probably were able to cross it in a raft or dugout canoe. Of course, it's also possible that they came instead from the south by traveling along the Ryukyu Islands. Also, since the Strait of Tartary and the La Pérouse Strait were both completely dry, it would have been possible to walk onto the Japanese archipelago by reaching the island of Hokkaido from the north, although this would have necessitated a bit of a detour through northeast Asia.

A: Because it was during a glacial period, doesn't that mean the climate was much colder than it is today? What would people's lives have been like?

B: It's true that temperatures would have generally been quite low. And because the Tsushima Strait was extremely narrow at the time, which restricted the flow of the Tsushima Warm Current, the climate of the Sea of Japan coast would likely have been especially cold. On the flip side, winters then would probably not have been as snowy as they are today. This is because, without the influence of the Tsushima Warm Current, sea surface temperatures would necessarily have been lower. Therefore, there would have been less evaporation, and no matter how often the northwesterly monsoon winds might have blown in winter, this would have limited the generation of snow-bearing clouds. Similarly, there would have been less rainfall over the Japanese archipelago overall, and forests would have been dominated by conifers and deciduous trees that are well suited to a cold, dry climate. Compared to today's forests, these past forests would have been less productive; so, it's hard to imagine that there was all that much food.

A: So . . . I guess you couldn't really call it a paradise. By the way, I've heard that the internal circulation of the Sea of Japan was very different during the glacial period compared to how it is today.

B: That's a very important point. At the same time that the decline in sea level narrowed the Tsushima Strait and restricted the inflow of the Tsushima Warm Current, the Sea of Japan continued to receive freshwater input from various rivers. These two factors combined to decrease surface-water salinity in the Sea of Japan. In fact, around 15,000–20,000 years ago, at the point when the climate was coldest, surface-water salinity in the Sea of Japan is thought to have declined to around two-thirds of what it is today. Do you know what happens when the salinity of the surface water decreases?

A: Yes. The surface water becomes less dense. Eventually, it becomes so much less dense that no matter how strongly it is cooled in winter, it cannot gain enough density to sink into the deep sea. As a result, the Sea of Japan becomes less vertically mixed. In fact, scientists can tell from examining seafloor sediment records that the supply of oxygen to the deep ocean sometimes became so weak that the bottom water became anoxic.

B: You're exactly right! The deep water of the Sea of Japan became a "dead zone" just as in the present-day Black Sea. Despite the name, however, there would still have been some fish in the surface waters thanks to the oxygen produced by photosynthesis.

A: I'm feeling pretty grateful to our ancestors who had to survive the harsh conditions of the glacial period. But the environment must have become more livable once the glacial period ended and the interglacial period began, right?

B: Yes. Sea levels rose again, and about 8000 years ago, the Tsushima Warm Current started to flow into the Sea of Japan in earnest. That was the turning point. The Sea of Japan became a treasure trove of life, and Jomon culture began to flourish. Well, let's save that topic for another time.

A: Okay. Thank you, professor.

≋

5-2
The Wellspring of a Wealthy Country: The Role of the Sea of Japan

The Jomon period began approximately 16,000 years ago and lasted until 3000 years ago. The beginning of this time period was toward the end of the last glacial period, when global temperatures were beginning to rise. As glaciers melted, global sea levels rose until by 6000 years ago, they were basically the same as they are today. This higher sea level also meant that the Tsushima and Tsugaru Straits expanded to nearly their current widths and depths.

Beginning around 8000 years ago, the Tsushima Warm Current began to flow through the Tsushima Strait in earnest and dramatically altered the environments of the Sea of Japan and the Japanese archipelago. The arrival of this warm-water current from the south not only accelerated the warming of the Sea of Japan coast but also activated the "natural desalination device" that is responsible for high wintertime snowfall totals on the Japanese archipelago (see fig. 1-6)

These high wintertime snowfall totals are in large part responsible for the abundance of water on the Japanese archipelago. Of course, rainfall during the wet season and from typhoons also plays a part, but the relatively steep terrain of the Japanese archipelago limits their effect on water storage. This is because much of the water that falls during large rain events quickly flows back into the sea through rivers and streams.

Snow, however, does not behave in the same way. Instead of flowing into the sea, much of it piles up on the ground. This is especially true in mountainous regions, where the snowpack may last until spring or, at high altitudes, until summer. Then, the accumulated snow melts gradually into rivers and streams, moistening the soil or, in some cases, seeping into groundwater, which can persist underground for many years. For example, Jing Zhang and Hiroshi Satake, both of the University of Toyama, showed that the groundwater that wells up from the seabed in Toyama Bay originates as subsoil water high up in the Tateyama peaks of Japan's Northern Alps.

By analyzing levels of tritium (a radioisotope of hydrogen with a half-life of 12.3 years) contained in the upwelling groundwater, they found that it takes 10–20 years for the water to flow from the mountains to the sea. Tritium has a mass number of 3, and is sometimes written as ^{3}H or T. A substantial amount of the tritium that is currently detectable in the environment was produced during atmospheric nuclear tests conducted by the United States and Soviet Union in the 1960s.

Once released into the atmosphere, tritium replaces hydrogen atoms in water vapor (i.e., H_2O) and can then fall to the ground as rain or snow. Once this water soaks into the ground, the quantity of tritium declines at a rate corresponding to its half-life of 12.3 years. Therefore, the amount of tritium remaining in a sample of groundwater indicates how many years the sample has spent underground.

Groundwater is typically rich in nutrients, which are sometimes referred to as dissolved minerals. Thanks to the fresh water generated by the Sea of Japan's "natural desalination device," the Japanese archipelago is rich in groundwater. This high-nutrient groundwater upwells into numerous springs that nurture the growth of lush forests. After the end of the last ice age, evergreen broadleaf forests, which are native to warm temperate climates, replaced the coniferous and deciduous forests that had predominated in Japan's previously cold, dry climate. These new forests slowly accumulated fertile soils, setting the groundwork for the Japanese archipelago to become the breadbasket region that it is today.

Today, the Japanese archipelago is blanketed in forests. The primeval beech forest in the Shirakami Mountains (fig. 5-2, plate 2) is even a designated World Heritage Site. In fact, forests currently account for almost two-thirds of Japan's land area. This proportion is the third highest among developed countries after Finland and Sweden.

Lush forests and rich soils also enhance the productivity of fishing grounds by increasing nutrient concentrations in river water and groundwater that flow into the sea.

Once again, it bears repeating that the Japanese archipelago owes its warm and humid climate and abundant water resources to the Sea of

FIGURE 5–2: Primeval beech forests in the Shirakami Mountains (Photo by Masami Goto /Aflo).

Japan, and more specifically to the effects of the Tsushima Warm Current and extremely cold winter monsoon winds.

5-3
Jomon Culture and the Sea of Japan

The Jomon people survived and thrived off of the fruits, nuts, and berries produced by the Japanese archipelago's rich natural environment. These food resources also fed game animals, which no doubt became a source of food in their own right. Meanwhile, as the Sea of Japan became more vertically mixed, it became easier for nutrient-rich deep water to upwell to the surface. This fertilization would have increased productivity in the surface waters, thereby facilitating a plentiful supply of fish and shellfish.

In this way, the Jomon people found themselves in an environment where food could easily be obtained from both land and sea;

these conditions provided a solid foundation for Jomon culture to blossom. Yet the Sea of Japan also had a dark side: from time to time, it afflicted our ancestors (including the Jomon people and their successors) with hardship.

Especially in winter, strong northwesterly monsoon winds would blow across the Sea of Japan and blanket nearly the entire coastline in a heavy layer of snow. Snowfalls have been a source of hardship in the past, and they remain so today: in the countryside, heavy snowfalls can block roads and destroy buildings.

In fact, life in the Japanese archipelago is beset by natural disasters today just as it was for our ancestors. These disasters include not just snow but earthquakes, tsunamis, volcanic eruptions, and typhoons. At times, the Jomon people would have been helpless in the face of these overwhelming natural forces. In these moments, the very concept of being able to tame and confront nature would have become unthinkable. Instead, over the 10,000 years of the Jomon period, these disasters may have reinforced a tendency to accept and seek to live in harmony with the natural world. This belief, perpetuated over the millennia, eventually became foundational to Japanese culture.

The Jomon people as well as their successors had to accumulate various skills to survive the fickleness of the natural world. They had to help each other in times of crisis, construct more durable dwellings, and store food in preparation for periods of scarcity. These challenges would have steeled their spirits and cultivated a contemplative mindset. The incredible pillar-supported buildings and numerous clay and wooden artifacts discovered in the Sannai-Maruyama Historical Site (4200 to 5900 years ago) in Aomori Prefecture, among others, are a testament to the culture they developed through their strong will to live.

You could even say that the basic character and sensibility of Japanese culture developed and matured during the Jomon period. I believe that the presence of the Sea of Japan alongside the Jomon people during this time played a larger role than many have imagined. What would have happened if the Sea of Japan did not exist? Each time I consider this question, I am more convinced of the Sea of Japan's fundamental importance.

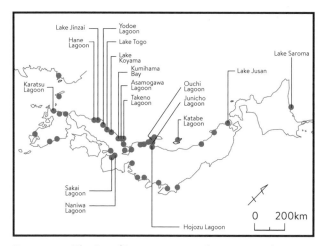

FIGURE 5-3: The Sea of Japan coast contains numerous lagoons, which make good natural harbors (from Mori, 1993). Some of the lagoons indicated in the figure have been filled in by land reclamation or natural sediment deposition and no longer exist.

5-4
The Development of the Sea of Japan Cultural Region

The Sea of Japan was also important in the establishment of trade routes. Beginning in the Jomon period, the people of the region made extensive use of the Sea of Japan for trade and cultural exchange. Over time, this led to the development of what is known as the "Sea of Japan Cultural Region," which was first discovered by archeologists and cross-cultural-studies researchers.

In Japan, the coast of the Sea of Japan contains numerous lagoons, as shown in figure 5-3. This is because the terrain and environmental conditions of the Sea of Japan coast seem to favor lagoon formation. For example, strong wintertime monsoon winds along the Sea of Japan coast can create spits (long sand or gravel bars extending from the shoreline and formed by strong coastal currents that transport sediment along the seabed) and harbor bars (spits that reach nearly all the way across the mouth of a bay or inlet). Either of these coastal formations can separate a body of water from the larger ocean, creating a lagoon.

As pointed out by the archaeologist Koichi Mori, these lagoons were often used as natural harbors and may have played a large role in the development of maritime shipping routes in the ancient Sea of Japan (Mori, 1993). Of course, once these lagoons became central to maritime shipping routes, they attracted a growing population that settled in their vicinity. In fact, many of these lagoons became population centers in ancient city-states. Gradually, more and more ships were moored in these ports, and trade routes extended not only within the Japanese archipelago but also to the Eurasian continent, facilitating the exchange of people and goods across the Sea of Japan. It seems likely that the introduction of new technologies and knowledge from abroad, as well as the increased rate of immigration, would have substantially accelerated the development of Japanese culture.

In other words, whereas the Sea of Japan is in one way a buffer between two landmasses, with the use of appropriate means of transport it can also function as a medium for the mass exchange of people, goods, and knowledge. The fact that trade and cultural exchange was frequently occurring across the ancient Sea of Japan has been demonstrated by numerous archeological excavations.

For example, one object that is often found in ancient sites is a type of jewelry known as *ketsu* earrings or ornaments. The oldest *ketsu* earrings have been excavated in northeastern China and date to about 8000 years ago. The presence of these earrings in various regions of the Japanese archipelago around 5000–7000 years ago (during the Jomon period) indicate that they were also quite popular in Japan. This strongly suggests the presence of active maritime trade routes across the Sea of Japan.

Similarly, archeologists have also focused on another ancient accessory: jade earrings and other jade ornaments known as *taishu*. During the Jomon period, almost all jade in the Japanese archipelago was quarried in the Hime and Omi Rivers in present-day Itoigawa City, Niigata Prefecture, on the Sea of Japan coast. Yet ornaments made from this jade have been found in Jomon period sites across the Japanese archipelago from the island of Hokkaido in the north to Kyushu in the south.

Much later, during the Kofun period from the mid-third century to the end of the seventh century, jade *magatama* beads were also used in sites on the Korean Peninsula. These are also thought to have been transported to the Korean Peninsula through maritime trade routes across the Sea of Japan.

≈

5-5
The Sea of Japan as a Hub for International Exchange

The historical record shows how the Sea of Japan Cultural Region expanded and prospered as the Sea of Japan became a hub for international exchange. People from the Korean Peninsula and regions to its northeast cleverly used ocean currents and monsoon winds to help them sail to the Japanese archipelago. They brought with them not only goods but also new and advanced cultures and technologies.

For example, envoys from the Korean kingdom of Goguryeo frequently traveled around the Sea of Japan during the sixth and seventh centuries. The first official envoy from Goguryeo visited Japan in the year 516. The envoys used the Tsushima Warm Current to speed up their journey across the Sea of Japan and often made landfall in the Koshi region (present-day Niigata, Toyama, and Ishikawa Prefectures). The frequency of their arrivals was such that an overland route was established to facilitate their travel from the city of Tsuruga to the Yamato region (around present-day Nara Prefecture) via Lake Biwa and the Yodo River.

At the time, the Korean Peninsula was occupied by three kingdoms: Baekje, Silla, and Goguryeo. All three of these kingdoms are known to have sent frequent diplomatic missions to Japan. Japan had friendly diplomatic relations with the Baekje kingdom but was often in conflict with

Silla. Goguryeo also had a hostile relationship with the kingdom of Silla and sought to restrain Silla's ambitions by forming an alliance with Japan.

China was the major continental power at the time (during the Sui and Tang dynasties) and had an extremely dynamic and volatile relationship with the kingdoms of the Korean Peninsula; the region could be described as a "tinderbox" during much of this period. Eventually, the Tang dynasty entered into an alliance with Silla, which conquered the Baekje kingdom in the year 663 and Goguryeo in the year 668. This gave the kingdom of Silla control over the entire Korean Peninsula.

During this conflict, Japanese forces seeking to aid the kingdom of Baekje suffered a defeat at the hands of the Tang dynasty in the Battle of Baekgang. Japan also became a destination for many refugees seeking to escape the frequent wars on the Korean Peninsula.

While East Asia plunged into conflict and warfare, Japan was able to maintain its independence, provide safe harbor to refugees from the continent, and continue to adopt new cultures and technologies. This isolation from the turbulent history of the continent was due in no small part to the "buffer" provided by the Sea of Japan.

5-6
A Calendar from the Balhae Kingdom

One particularly well-known example of international exchange across the Sea of Japan occurred between Japan and the Balhae kingdom (a successor to the Goguryeo kingdom, it was originally named Jin and lasted from 698 to 926) in the eighth to tenth centuries. After the first envoy from Balhae landed in the Ezo region of the Japanese archipelago (present-day Hokkaido) in 727, Japan dispatched its first envoy across the Sea of Japan to the Balhae kingdom the very next year, in 728. Although the sending of Japanese envoys to the Balhae kingdom ended after the 15th diplomatic mission in the year 811, the Balhae kingdom continued to send envoys to Japan until 929, when they sent their 34th diplomatic mission.

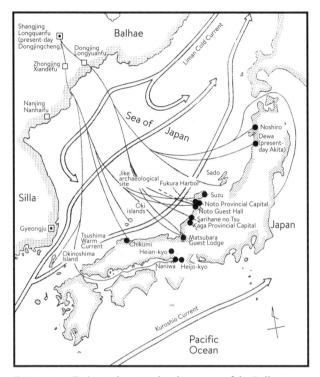

FIGURE 5-4: *Estimated route taken by envoys of the Balhae kingdom (modified from Takase, 1984).*

Figure 5-4 shows potential routes that these envoys may have taken between Japan and the Balhae kingdom. Envoys from the Balhae kingdom made use of northwesterly monsoon winds that blow across the Sea of Japan from autumn to winter to reach the coast of Japan, and then followed the Tsushima Warm Current to arrive at a harbor.

On the return journey, the Balhae envoys seem to have traveled north across the Sea of Japan in April–August and then followed the Liman Cold Current to the coast of the Balhae kingdom. They were skilled navigators, and the routes they followed clearly show that they had an empirical understanding of currents in the Sea of Japan.

At the beginning of the diplomatic relationship between the two countries, the Balhae kingdom sought to ally itself with Japan, as both countries were in conflict with Silla at the time. However, tensions with Silla soon eased and the focus of the alliance shifted away from military concerns. Instead, the relationship became much more about trade and cultural exchange.

Items that were brought into Japan from the Balhae kingdom include the fur and skins of martens, brown bears, leopards, and tigers, as well as carrots, honey, ceramics, Buddhist altar fittings, and scriptures. Items that were traded in the other direction include high-quality textiles such as silk fabrics, gold and mercury, handicrafts, camellia oil, and lacquer made from the sap of the *Acanthopanax sciadophylloides* tree. Silk products are said to have been especially prized in the Balhae kingdom, where conditions were not favorable for silkworm breeding.

During this era, an extremely important piece of writing from the Tang dynasty arrived in Japan for the first time: this is the Xuanming calendar, which was brought to Japan by an envoy from the Balhae kingdom in the year 859. The Xuanming calendar is an extremely accurate lunisolar calendar developed in Tang-dynasty China. In Japan, it was used during the years 862–1684, a time period of some 822 years lasting until the middle of the Edo period, and proved to be a reliable way to tie people's daily lives to the passage of time.

≈

5-7
Kitamae *Ships: The Backbone of Domestic Trade*

Some of you may be familiar with *kitamae* ships. This is a generic term for wooden Japanese-style sailing ships that transported and sold goods between the Ezo region and Osaka during the mid-Edo to Meiji periods (from around 1750 to 1900).

More specifically, the single-masted Japanese ships that played a major role during the Edo period are known as *bezai* or *sengoku* ships

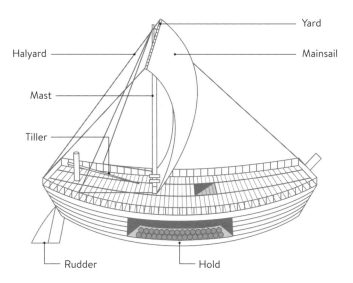

Yard

Halyard

Mainsail

Mast

Tiller

Rudder

Hold

FIGURE 5-5: Structure of a bezai *ship. The hold was packed full of goods in straw bags. The halyard was used to raise and lower the mainsail, and the rudder was operated using a tiller.*

(fig. 5-5). The *bezai* ship is a unique cargo ship that was developed during this period. The Edo shogunate (established in 1603) implemented an isolationist policy known as *sakoku* that greatly restricted interactions with other countries. However, this policy had the secondary effect of promoting domestic trade.

Bezai ships were designed to quickly transport a large volume of goods at the lowest possible cost. As seamanship and shipbuilding skills gradually improved, by the 1700s most *bezai* ships were able to sail into headwinds without the use of oars. This proved enormously useful because it saved labor costs that would otherwise have been needed to hire rowers. Large *bezai* ships with a carrying capacity of several hundred to over 1000 stones (approximately 150 t) crisscrossed the Seto Inland Sea and the waters around Japan and became a major factor in the growth of domestic industries and the transport of goods.

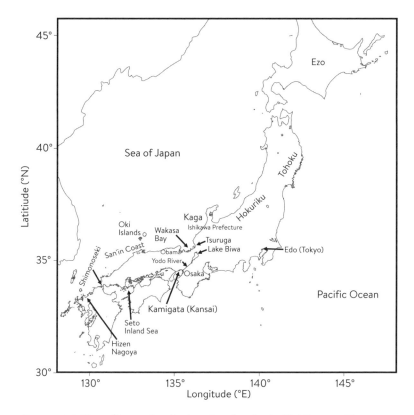

FIGURE 5–6: Map of Japan showing locations involved with kitamae ships.

5-8
The Maeda Clan of the Kaga Domain Pioneered Shipping in the Sea of Japan

To reach the Kamigata region (present-day Kansai) from the Sea of Japan, envoys from the Goguryeo and Balhae kingdoms had to travel over land from Wakasa Bay via Lake Biwa and the Yodo River (fig. 5-6).

This land route remained a major transport route for goods until the early Edo period, and cities such as Tsuruga and Obama, which face Wakasa Bay, flourished as stops along this route. Goods from the Ezo, Tohoku, and Hokuriku regions were carried by ship across the Sea of Japan to Tsuruga or Obama, after which they were transferred onto the overland route.

However, when Toyotomi Hideyoshi dispatched troops to Korea (1592–1598), a base of operations was established in Hizen-Nagoya (in northern Saga Prefecture) on the island of Kyushu. The Maeda clan of the Kaga Domain (present-day Ishikawa Prefecture) was forced to assemble a fleet to send a large contingent of troops and rice provisions down the San'in coast to Kyushu. As a result, they pioneered the transport of goods through the Sea of Japan.

During the Edo period in the mid-seventeenth century, the Maeda clan also established the *kitamae* shipping route, this time for commercial use. Instead of using the overland route from Tsuruga, this new route facilitated transport of the rice needed to pay an annual rice tax entirely by sea down the San'in coast to Shimonoseki and then through the Seto Inland Sea to Osaka (the main city of the Kansai region).

The benefits of this route included the ability to move larger volumes of rice at one time and the lack of transshipment, which cut down on costs and labor. Various other clans gradually took note of these advantages and began to adopt this route for their own use. Eventually, the route became standard not only for transporting the annual rice tax from each fiefdom but also for a variety of products carried by private shipping firms.

The core of the *kitamae* ships' business was made up of seafood products such as herring, salmon, and kelp from the Ezo region and other goods such as rice, salt, sake, and cotton from Osaka. The relatively calm waters of the Sea of Japan (except in winter) were well suited for transporting large volumes of goods, and this became a mainstay of Japanese commercial activity. It is quite plausible that this shipping route not only contributed to the development of a commodity economy but also encouraged information distribution throughout Japan and hastened the development of the Ezo region. Many ports along the Sea of Japan coast and in the Seto Inland Sea flourished as ports of call for the *kitamae* ships.

The French explorer La Pérouse, who I introduced in section 3-1, recounted an encounter with two *kitamae* ships off the coast of the Oki Islands in the Sea of Japan in his account of his voyages around the world. You can read about this encounter in the column at the end of this chapter.

The era of Japanese-style sailing ships came to an end around the middle of the Meiji period. Land-based communications and transport networks greatly expanded their reach, making the *kitamae* ships increasingly redundant. Yet the Sea of Japan remains an important conduit for transportation even today. In fact, large ferries frequently carry people and vehicles between the islands of Hokkaido and Honshu. There is no doubt that this use of the Sea of Japan will continue into the future.

≋

5-9
Lessons from the Sea of Japan for the Next Generation

Throughout history, the Sea of Japan has been an important arena for maritime trade. It could be said that its importance equals that of the Mediterranean in fostering a cooperative society involving multiple nations. Up until the Meiji period, the Sea of Japan was referred to, and also functioned as, Japan's "front door."

However, over the past 150 years or so, the center of gravity of Japan's culture and economy has shifted to Tokyo and the Pacific coast. Figure 5-7 shows the populations of five prefectures that border the Pacific Ocean (including Tokyo) and five prefectures that border the Sea of Japan from 1920 to 2010. There is a clear difference between the two sides of the Japanese archipelago. Whereas the trend in population is almost flat on the Sea of Japan side, the population on the Pacific side has increased several-fold.

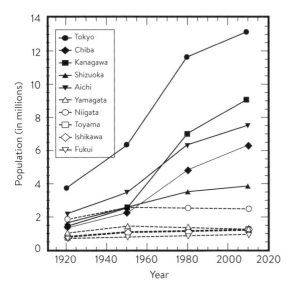

Figure 5–7: Trends in population from 1920 to 2010 in five prefectures that border the Pacific Ocean (filled symbols) and five prefectures that border the Sea of Japan (open symbols). Source: Census data from the Ministry of Internal Affairs and Communications.

Starting in the Meiji period (1868–1912), the Pacific coast became increasingly Westernized and its economy blossomed through a strong emphasis on mass production and consumption. This relegated the Sea of Japan to the status of Japan's "other sea." In fact, at one point, the Pacific coast even took on the moniker of Japan's "front side," whereas the Sea of Japan coast became known as the "other side." To my mind, the population trends shown in figure 5-7 are a stark reminder of this shift.

Yet in today's society where sustainability has become an increasingly urgent issue, it may be time to reevaluate the Sea of Japan coast. We must recognize that natural resources are finite and mass consumption is incompatible with sustainability. Instead, we need to turn our attention to resource conservation and recycling.

Perhaps, in our current time, the Sea of Japan should be looked upon as a symbol of sustainable values and coexistence with the natural environment. Throughout history, people living in the Sea of Japan region have been conscious of it as a small, limited space. Surely, this must have driven them to cultivate the skills and knowledge needed to maintain a balance between humans and nature, and to understand how to interact with the ocean while ensuring that the benefits it provides will last indefinitely.

Although it aired a long time ago, I still remember a TV program on NHK (Japan's national broadcaster) that illustrates how this knowledge persists among the residents of the Sea of Japan coast. This was a program entitled *Negai nite: Niigata-ken Sado-shi* (From Negai: Sado City, Niigata Prefecture) in the *Chiisana Tabi* (A Small Journey) series, which was broadcast in May 2012.

In the program, the television presenter Sachiko Kagami visits a small village named Negai (Japanese for "hope") in Sado City, Niigata Prefecture, for the first time since a visit 16 years before. In April, during the peak of the *wakame* seaweed harvesting season, she meets a woman she once knew who even now, at the age of 84, continues to work on the water. When this woman talks about what she calls "the ocean of Negai" (the Sea of Japan), her passion for the place is evident in her voice.

What struck me was this: how keenly the woman was aware of the limits to the ocean's resources, the importance of not harvesting too much at once, and the need to be efficient in what you use. The TV cameras captured the woman's delight as she interacted with her sons and daughters who had been away from the island. I still can't forget the joy on the faces of the village residents and the ways in which they helped each other and shared what they could with one another.

I will leave you with one more example. The city of Himi in Toyama Prefecture is working to teach their traditional method of fixed-net fishing to fishers in developing countries such as Thailand and Indonesia. The Etchu *daibo ami* technique is a fixed-net fishing method with a 400-year history in Himi. In contrast to more modern methods that seek to catch as many fish as possible, this technique allows fishers to catch only the required amount of fish of a particular size. It is a technique that is rooted in the idea of sustainable use.

There are countless examples of such techniques being used in the Sea of Japan region. Taken together, they are evidence of a mindset that has persisted throughout the history of the Sea of Japan, where people have had to make efficient use of limited resources. If we could only shine more light on this mindset premised on the small size of the "mini-ocean," it might prompt us to appreciate the Sea of Japan more fully. It is my sincere hope that these values and attitudes might one day spread not just within Japan but also internationally and start a strong movement toward environmental protection and the creation of sustainable societies.

~~~~~~~~~~~~~ Column 5 ~~~~~~~~~~~~~

When La Pérouse Encountered *Kitamae* Ships in the Sea of Japan

You may remember La Pérouse from chapter 3. He was the first Western explorer to enter the Sea of Japan, and his account of his voyages popularized the name "Sea of Japan" in the Western world.

During his voyages, La Pérouse reported his fleet of two frigates encountering some peculiar Japanese ships. After passing into the Sea of Japan through the Tsushima Strait on 2 June 1787, the fleet was nearing the Oki Ridge (located roughly midway between the words "MER" and "DU" in the phrase "MER DU JAPON" on fig. 3-1) when two Japanese *kitamae* ships were sighted approaching from up ahead.

Photography had not yet been invented, and so it fell to Ensign Blondella to skillfully sketch these ships. These sketches can still be found in an appendix of La Pérouse's *Voyage de La Pérouse Autour du Monde* pt. 16–22 (translated by Tadao Kobayashi).

One of the two ships was a standard *bezai* ship as shown in figure 5-5, but the other (fig. 5-8) was of a completely different style.

According to Kenji Ishii and Hiroyuki Adachi, both authorities on historical Japanese ships, the second ship is the *Sangoku Maru*, a 1500-stone ship that had just gone into service the

FIGURE 5-8: *A sketch of the ship* Sangoku Maru *encountered by La Pérouse (from* Voyage de La Pérouse Autour du Monde.

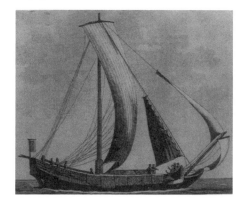

~~~~~~~~~~~~~~~~~~~~ *Column 5* ~~~~~~~~~~~~~~~~~~~~

previous October (Ishii, 1995b; Adachi, 1998). The name "Sangoku" (three nations) derives from its hybrid design, which sought to combine the merits of three shipbuilding traditions: Japanese, Chinese, and Western (or more specifically in this case, Dutch).

For example, the ship featured a Japanese-style turret atop a hull built in the style of a Chinese junk, with a Japanese central mainsail flanked by Western-style auxiliary sails (including triangular sails) at the bow and stern.

The purpose of the ship was to transport dried and straw-wrapped products such as sea cucumbers, abalone, and shark fins from Matsumae (in northern Japan) to Nagasaki. These were important export products for the Chinese (Qing dynasty) market.

By adopting a hybrid design, the shipbuilders aimed to create a more durable and maneuverable ship. The *bezai* ships were strictly designed for use in protected waters, and were unsuited for the rough conditions of the Sea of Japan in winter. With the *Sangoku Maru*, however, it was hoped that the ship would be able to weather these conditions at sea, meaning that there would no longer be any need to seek shelter in a harbor and wait for favorable weather. This would shave days off the length of the voyage and allow the ship to make two round trips a year, potentially garnering huge profits for its operators. When La Pérouse's fleet encountered the *Sangoku Maru*, it was during the calm summer months, and the passage far offshore of the Sea of Japan coast would have been a speedy one.

The *Voyage de La Pérouse Autour du Monde* contains an interesting description of the encounter:

"We passed close enough to see the faces of the Japanese sailors, but their expressions showed neither fear nor surprise. . . . We called out to them as we passed, but they did not understand our questions, and we were unable to comprehend their answers. The Japanese vessels continued to voyage southward."

These words contain a palpable sense of disappointment.

The *Sangoku Maru* would have been heavily loaded with cargo at the time, and its crew must have been shocked to find themselves approached not just by a foreign vessel but a warship to boot. Afraid that a bad interaction would endanger the cargo, one could speculate that the crew may have feigned indifference in an effort to depart the area as amicably as possible.

The *Sangoku Maru* was the only "hybrid" ship operating in Japan at the time. The fact that this singular ship encountered La Pérouse's fleet in the middle of the Sea of Japan, and that a precise sketch was created during this meeting and survives to the present day, is nothing short of a miracle.

A cruel fate awaited the *Sangoku Maru* in its subsequent travels. In September 1788, one year after encountering La Pérouse's fleet, the *Sangoku Maru* was sailing south from Hakodate through the Sea of Japan when it was hit by a storm (perhaps, based on the season, a typhoon) off the Noto Peninsula. Although the crew managed to escape on a *tenma* boat (the equivalent of a lifeboat today), the *Sangoku Maru* drifted ashore and broke apart at Akaishi Beach in Dewa Province (in present-day Akita Prefecture).

After less than two years of service, it seems unlikely that it had managed to earn back the cost of its initial construction. In the aftermath of this incident, the shogunate changed its policies around shipbuilding, and a ship of this type was never built again.

| Chapter 6 |

A Warning from the "Miniature Ocean": The Sea of Japan's Lament

Human impacts on the environment have vastly expanded in scale since the beginning of the Industrial Revolution. Today, these impacts span the globe and include the ongoing issue of global climate change.

These impacts pose a particular risk to Japan. For example, any weakening of northwesterly winter monsoon winds could threaten the functioning of the Sea of Japan's "natural desalination device," which is a central pillar of Japan's water supply.

Other changes are already being observed. For example, dissolved-oxygen concentrations in Japan Sea Bottom Water have declined by 10% over the past 30 years. This decline likely reflects a slowdown in the Sea of Japan's thermohaline circulation caused by recent changes in climate.

The "miniature ocean" is akin to a canary in a coal mine. Now is the time to take the signs of its distress seriously and consider what needs to be done to protect the environment of the Sea of Japan and of all the world's oceans.

6-1
The Increasing Severity of Global Climate Change

The Intergovernmental Panel on Climate Change (IPCC) published its latest comprehensive climate report (the Fifth Assessment Report) in 2013–14. Its findings leave no doubt that global climate change and other climate perturbations are caused by ongoing human activities.

Studies have shown that atmospheric concentrations of greenhouse gases including carbon dioxide and methane have rapidly increased since the Industrial Revolution. This can be seen by comparing the current concentrations of these gases in the atmosphere against those in samples of the atmosphere in the past as preserved in polar ice cores. Greenhouse gases contribute to climate warming by absorbing a portion of the infrared rays reflected by the Earth's surface and preventing this energy from escaping into space. In other words, they work somewhat like an insulating blanket covering the Earth.

The atmospheric concentration of carbon dioxide, for example, was around 280 parts per million (0.028%) before the Industrial Revolution. When I was a student, we were taught that carbon dioxide accounted for around 0.03% of the atmosphere. In the span of just one generation, this number has risen to over 0.04%.

Scientists have also used observed temperature records to show that the increase in greenhouse-gas concentrations has been accompanied by a rise in surface temperatures around the world (fig. 6-1).

In January 2015, the National Aeronautics and Space Administration and the National Oceanic and Atmospheric Administration, both of the United States, announced that the world's average temperature in the preceding year had been the highest since 1880, when records began.

Scientists have used supercomputers running highly detailed models to project that average global temperatures will rise by 1–4°C by the end of this century. This is not to say that each region of the world can expect the same magnitude of temperature increase. High-latitude regions, for example, are expected to warm at faster rates than the global average.

In polar regions, this faster warming is likely to accelerate the

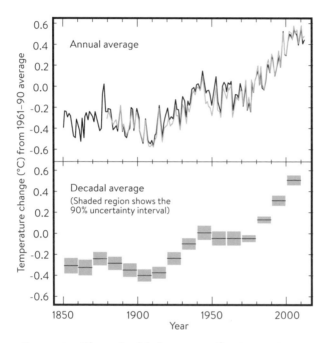

FIGURE 6-1: *Change in global average surface temperature from 1850 to 2012. Changes in temperature are shown relative to the 1961–90 average, which includes observations over both land and sea. One-year averages (top panel) were calculated for multiple datasets. Modified with permission from the Intergovernmental Panel on Climate Change, Working Group I, Fifth Assessment Report, Summary for Policy Makers, Figure SPM.1(a) (IPCC, 2013).*

melting of sea ice and glaciers. A decline in summer sea-ice extent is already being observed in the Arctic Ocean, and some experts believe that a commercial shipping route (the Northeast Passage) may soon open up. Additionally, the melting of glaciers is a major contributor to sea-level rise (global sea levels are expected to rise by about 1 m by the end of this century). This means that as the glaciers melt, coastlines will move inland in many regions, and some low-lying islands will even become entirely submerged.

Scientists also believe that changing surface temperatures may have serious global effects on ocean circulation patterns, ocean–atmosphere fluxes, and rates of heat exchange between high and low latitudes. If surface temperatures rise in high-latitude oceans, this may inhibit the formation of high-density surface waters and reduce downwelling into the deep sea, slowing down Broecker's ocean conveyor belt (see chapter 2). It is critical that we gain a good understanding of how the global thermohaline circulation may change in the future, and how these changes will affect seawater chemistry and ocean ecology around the world.

I have already explained that the Sea of Japan is extremely sensitive to changes in environmental conditions. In fact, it functions as a kind of "canary in a coal mine," or early warning system, for changes that may soon occur on a much broader scale. In these next sections, I will describe how this "miniature ocean" is already in the early stages of several environmental shifts.

≈

6-2
Changes in Japan Sea Bottom Water

My first research cruise in the Sea of Japan was in September–October 1977. This was my fourth time aboard the *Hakuho Maru*; I had already gotten to know the crew and had become accustomed to the work of oceanographic observation.

As I mentioned in sections 3-6 and 3-7, we selected sampling locations across the three major basins of the Sea of Japan (the Japan, Yamato, and Tsushima Basins; see fig. 1-2), and at each location we lowered water samplers on steel cables to collect seawater from a range of depths. I was in charge of analyzing dissolved-oxygen concentrations in the collected seawater samples after they were brought aboard the ship.

To determine dissolved-oxygen concentrations, I used a simple titration method known as the Winkler test, which was first developed more than 100 years ago. The method works by producing a solution with an iodine concentration that is directly proportional to the oxygen concentration of the sample.

One disadvantage of this method is that iodine is a volatile substance that can easily escape into the air, meaning that any iodine that is lost during the process of analysis will skew the results toward lower oxygen concentrations. I had noticed this problem during a research cruise the previous year and had devised an improved measurement method in preparation for this, my first research cruise in the Sea of Japan; I created a new glass bottle for sealing seawater samples and in which to evolve iodine to be titrated. The ability to use the sample bottle as the titration vessel is a big advantage; it prevents iodine loss during sample transfer from a sample bottle to another vessel as was conventionally done at that time.

Based on what I had read and what I had heard from senior researchers, I was expecting that the Sea of Japan would be rich in oxygen (see fig. 2-5). Also, as I mentioned in section 3-11, I knew that Japan Sea Bottom Water, which is found at depths below about 2000 m, is an extremely uniform water mass with very little variation in temperature. I successfully analyzed the seawater samples and was very happy with my results. They showed that bottom-water oxygen concentrations were clearly higher than in the western North Pacific, and that oxygen concentrations in Japan Sea Bottom Water are just as uniform as temperature.

Two years later, in June–August 1979, I had the opportunity to analyze new samples aboard the *Hakuho Maru* that had been collected at almost the same locations in the Sea of Japan. Once again, I relied on the exact same method to measure dissolved oxygen. Since it had only been two years since the last measurement, I was confident that little would have changed.

Yet when I compared the new data to the numbers from two years before, I couldn't believe my eyes. The two vertical profiles were similar, but clearly not identical. Whereas the average bottom-water oxygen concentration in September 1977 was 230 μmol/kg (n = 7 data points), it had fallen to 227 μmol/kg (n = 5 data points) in July 1979.

You may think this is a negligible difference, but for me as a chemist, a measurement error of over 1% in such a basic analytical procedure was simply unacceptable.

"Where could I have made a mistake?" I thought to myself. I was convinced that something had gone wrong. I carefully checked the glassware and reference standards to try to root out the source of the error and re-did the analysis again and again. But no matter what I did, I couldn't find the problem.

"It's just measurement error," is what I was told by those around me. But upon further consideration, I realized that the fact that measured oxygen concentrations were highly consistent within years (the standard deviation was ±1 µmol/kg or less in both 1977 and 1979) suggested that something else was happening. I was forced to conclude that the 3 µmol/kg difference between years reflected an actual change that had occurred in the ocean.

Generally, rates of oxygen supply and consumption in the deep sea are in balance and oxygen concentrations remain in a steady state. Therefore, multiple oxygen concentration measurements taken at different times should agree with one another to within the range of measurement error. In fact, when I analyzed past measurements of oxygen concentration in the deep water of the western North Pacific and the Philippine Sea, I found that measured oxygen concentrations had not changed at all during the past 10 or 20 years.

Yet in the Sea of Japan, I had measured a 3 µmol/kg decline over just two years. What in the world was going on?

6-3
A 10% Decline in Just 30 Years!

My mistake had been to assume that what was true of the global oceans would also be true of the Sea of Japan. As will be revealed later, rather than being surprising or improbable, my oxygen concentration

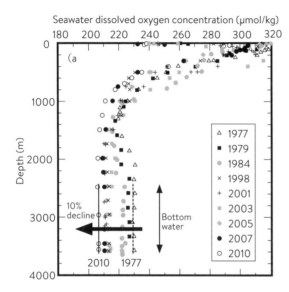

Seawater dissolved oxygen concentration (μmol/kg)

FIGURE 6-2: Declining oxygen concentrations in the bottom water of the Sea of Japan. Measurements were obtained in the eastern Japan Basin (41–42°N, 137–138°E) from 1977–2010 (Gamo et al., 2014).

measurements were in fact quite normal in the "miniature ocean." At the time, I did not yet understand why the Sea of Japan was different.

But five years later, in August 1984, I obtained the measurements that would make this clear once and for all. Once again, I was in the Sea of Japan aboard the *Hakuho Maru* collecting bottom-water samples from the same locations and analyzing them in the same manner as before. This time, the average oxygen concentration was just 223 μmol/kg!

At last, there was no room for doubt; the numbers were definitely declining. Yes, it turns out that unlike in the Pacific and other large oceans, the deep waters of the "miniature ocean" don't necessarily stay the same from year to year. This is true even of bottom waters pulled up from a depth of 3000 m.

After this, I continued to take measurements at the same locations whenever I got the chance. Figure 6-2 shows all of the dissolved-oxygen profiles that I have obtained so far.

These measurements show that bottom-water oxygen concentrations have continued to decline since 1977, reaching 207 μmol/kg in 2010.

This translates to a 23 μmol/kg decline in 33 years, which is exactly 10% of the oxygen concentration (230 μmol/kg) that I first measured in 1977. If this rate of decline were to continue into the future, oxygen concentrations would fall to zero in just 330 years.

This decline in bottom-water oxygen is not limited to the eastern Japan Basin. Similar declines have also been observed in the Yamato and Tsushima Basins. This indicates that this decline is occurring across almost the entire Sea of Japan.

Figure 6-3 shows yearly averages of just the bottom-water data over time. I have extended the time series past 1977 (my first oxygen measurements in the Sea of Japan) by incorporating as much data from the literature as possible; the earliest available data points are from around 1930.

Oxygen concentrations in the eastern Japan Basin are slightly higher than those in the Yamato Basin because the eastern Japan Basin is closer to the region where bottom water is generated and can more easily receive oxygen input from downwelling surface water.

In 1930, when Kanji Suda and Michitaka Uda first started conducting observations of the Sea of Japan in earnest (see section 3-7), bottom-water oxygen concentrations were around 250 μmol/kg. In the ensuing 80 years, oxygen concentrations declined by some 43 μmol/kg, or 17%.

≋

6-4
A Shortage of Income or Too Much Spending?

One way to think about the decline in bottom-water oxygen in the Sea of Japan is by comparing it to a household budget. In other words, the modern Sea of Japan is comparable to a household where spending (outgoing money) exceeds income (incoming money). In the case of the Sea of Japan, the "spending" is the amount of oxygen consumed by organic-matter decomposition in the bottom-water layer, and "income" is the amount of oxygen supplied by surface-water downwelling. Because the former exceeds the latter, "savings" (i.e., oxygen concentration) are gradually being lost.

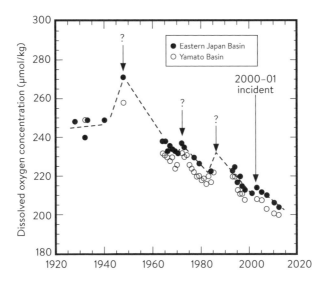

Figure 6-3: Changes in dissolved-oxygen concentration in the bottom water of the Sea of Japan. Data points show oxygen measurements obtained over the past 80 years in the Yamato Basin (unfilled circles) and eastern Japan Basin (filled circles).

As you may remember from previous sections, microorganisms consume oxygen in the deep sea by aerobically decomposing sinking organic matter. Because bottom waters are devoid of sunlight, oxygen cannot be generated locally by photosynthesis. This means that, in the absence of some other oxygen input, bottom-water oxygen concentrations would eventually decline to zero. As I described in the column at the end of chapter 1, this is true of the Black Sea today.

In principle, the Sea of Japan has a mechanism to replenish bottom-water oxygen: its thermohaline circulation, which involves the downwelling of oxygen-rich surface water. If this additional oxygen input balances out the rate of consumption, bottom-water oxygen should remain stable.

In recent times, however, oxygen concentrations have continued to fall. This means that input has not kept up with consumption. There are three ways in which this could have happened.

First, the rate of oxygen supply may have remained constant while the rate of oxygen consumption increased. Second, the rate of supply may have declined while consumption remained constant. In our earlier budget analogy, the first scenario is comparable to an increase in spending while income remains the same, while the second scenario is comparable to a decline in income while spending remains the same. Finally, it is also possible that oxygen supply and consumption both changed, but consumption exceeded supply. In any of these cases, the total amount of money (i.e., oxygen concentration) is bound to decrease.

6-5
Water Temperatures Are Also Rising

Let's consider the first scenario. If rates of photosynthetic activity increased in the surface waters of the Sea of Japan, this would boost biological production and increase the export of organic matter (e.g., marine snow) into deep water, thereby stimulating more oxygen consumption from aerobic decomposition. However, there is very little indication of a recent increase in nutrient input, biological production, or phytoplankton concentration in the surface waters of the Sea of Japan. In other words, there has probably been little to no increase in photosynthetic activity in the Sea of Japan in recent times.

Therefore, our attention should shift to the second scenario: that is, that oxygen input from surface-water downwelling has either slowed or stalled. Extremely cold wintertime air temperatures are required to form surface water of sufficient density to sink to the bottom of the Sea of Japan. Climate change is likely to inhibit this process by raising air temperatures, weakening northwesterly winter monsoon winds, or both.

In fact, the Japan Meteorological Agency's long-term temperature dataset, which stretches back to 1965, shows that bottom-water temperatures have increased in conjunction with the decline in oxygen

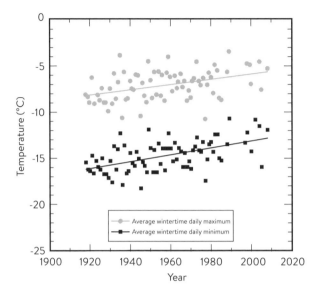

FIGURE 6–4: *Daily maximum and minimum temperatures in Vladivostok. Data points show average daily maximum (grey circles) and minimum (black squares) temperatures in winter (December–February) over the past 100 years.*

concentration. My own observations also show a 0.03°C increase between 1977 and 2007.

The seafloor contains a small but measurable amount of geothermal heat, which has the effect of warming the bottom-water layer. The fact that this heat source is having an increased effect on bottom-water temperatures is consistent with a weakening of cold and dense surface-water downwelling. In other words, the "household budget" is out of balance not just in terms of oxygen but heat as well.

What about wintertime air temperatures?

Let's take a look at air temperatures in Vladivostok, which is located near the region where surface-water downwelling occurs (fig. 6-4).

You can see that both maximum and minimum temperatures have

risen by about 3–4°C over the past century. Although this may include some urban heat-island effects (where anthropogenic forcings create higher temperatures in urban rather than rural environments), it is also reflective of the fact that climate change is expected to affect higher latitudes more severely. This explains why the 3–4°C increase observed in Vladivostok far outstrips the 0.8°C average temperature increase that has been observed globally during the twentieth century (see fig. 6-1).

This strong temperature rise is likely to have hindered wintertime surface-water cooling in the northern Sea of Japan. In addition, northwesterly wintertime monsoon winds appear to be weakening in recent years. These two factors combined may be enough to inhibit the formation of surface water with a sufficiently high density to sink into the deep sea and supply fresh oxygen to the bottom water of the Sea of Japan.

Could surface-water downwelling have stopped completely? Or is the surface water still sinking, but just not reaching the depth of the bottom-water layer?

≈

6-6
Something Is Wrong with the Sea of Japan's Thermohaline Circulation!

In section 5-2, I discussed how tritium (^3H or T) can be used to determine the age of groundwater. In this section, I will show how it can also provide important information on ocean circulation.

Tritium is a radionuclide with a half-life of 12.3 years. The only time it was intensively released into the atmosphere was during the 1960s, when it was produced during atmospheric nuclear tests and subsequently entered the ocean in the form of rainwater.

When surface waters sink into the deep sea, they add tritium to the deep- and bottom-water layers. In fact, surface waters that are in contact with the atmosphere are the only source of artificial tritium to the deep

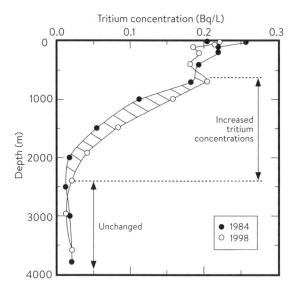

FIGURE 6–5: Changes in tritium concentration in the Sea of Japan. The two profiles show tritium concentrations measured in the eastern Japan Basin (41°21'N, 137°20'E) in 1984 and 1998. The 1998 data have been corrected to account for 14 additional years of radioactive decay relative to the 1984 data (Gamo et al., 2001).

sea. Moreover, tritium can only be transported along with water (H_2O) in the form of "THO" (a water molecule with one typical hydrogen atom replaced by tritium).

Taken together, these two facts mean that the following must also be true: increases in deep-water tritium concentration can only be caused by new surface-water downwelling.

Tritium concentrations in seawater samples collected from a single location during two separate years (1984 and 1998) are compared in figure 6-5.

Figure 6-5 provides two important insights:

On the one hand, tritium levels did not increase between 1984 and 1998 in the bottom-water layer (depths below ~2500 m). In other words, little to no surface water was able to sink into the bottom water during this 14-year period.

On the other hand, tritium levels did clearly increase at depths of 700–2000 m. This shows that surface-water downwelling was able to reach depths of up to, but no greater than, ~2500 m.

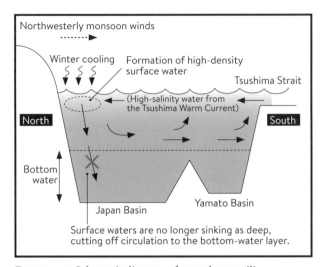

FIGURE 6–6: Schematic diagram of recently prevailing thermohaline circulation patterns in the Sea of Japan. Surface waters are no longer downwelling into the bottom-water layer, isolating the bottom water from the thermohaline circulation (Gamo et al., 2014). For comparison, see figure 1-7.

In chapter 1, I showed you a general schematic of thermohaline circulation in the Sea of Japan (fig. 1-7). The tritium data demonstrate that in recent years, the Sea of Japan has deviated from what I showed in this schematic. This new situation is represented in figure 6-6, which shows that surface waters are no longer sinking as deep as they did in the past. As a result, the bottom-water layer has become isolated from the thermohaline circulation.

Is today's Sea of Japan permanently locked into the situation shown in figure 6-6? Or will surface water of sufficient density to sink into the bottom water be generated at some point in the future?

≋

6-7
What Occurred in the Cold Winter of the Year 2000

Take another look at figure 6-3. You can clearly see that oxygen concentrations in Japan Sea Bottom Water are gradually declining. However, if you look closely, you will notice that the decline is not smooth.

Sometimes, oxygen concentrations seem to spike. These events are indicated by black arrows. After a brief interruption in the oxygen decline, the normal pattern resumes in subsequent years. In other words, new oxygen seems to have been supplied to the bottom water (albeit temporarily), meaning that new bottom water must have been formed. Is that really possible?

The short answer is yes. Oceanographic observations conducted immediately after the fact have confirmed that new bottom water was actually formed in the winter of 2000–01. That winter, the Sea of Japan experienced unusually cold temperatures.

In the early spring to summer of 2001, several research teams from Japan, Korea, Russia, and the United States took part in an oceanographic research cruise aboard a Russian vessel as part of the CREAMS project (see the column at the end of chapter 2). This voyage took them from the western Japan Basin to the Tsushima Basin.

By sheer luck, their observations captured an incredible event. Their data clearly show a high-oxygen water mass sliding down the slope of the seafloor offshore of Vladivostok at a depth of more than 3000 m (indicated by the thick arrow in fig. 6-7b). This water mass had not been present in the early spring of the previous year (fig. 6-7a). In addition to its high oxygen concentration, the water mass was characterized by low water temperature, high salinity, and low nutrient levels. This is clear evidence of new bottom-water formation in early 2001.

This newly downwelled bottom water would have mixed with surrounding water masses on its way to reaching the eastern Japan Basin and Yamato Basin in 2–3 years' time, whereupon it would have temporarily increased oxygen concentrations in these basins. This is the event marked "2000–01 incident" in figure 6-3.

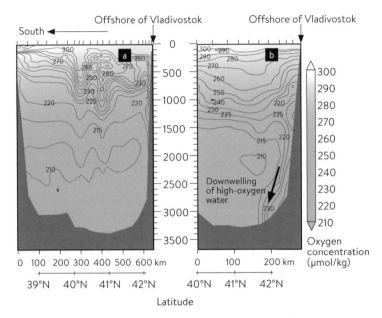

South ←

Offshore of Vladivostok

Offshore of Vladivostok

Downwelling
of high-oxygen
water

Oxygen
concentration
(μmol/kg)

0   100 200 300 400 500 600 km

0   100   200 km

39°N   40°N   41°N   42°N

40°N   41°N   42°N

Latitude

FIGURE 6-7: Dissolved-oxygen concentrations in the Sea of Japan along a vertical section running north–south from Vladivostok. Numbers in figure panels indicate oxygen concentrations in μmol/kg. Measurements were conducted on (a) 3–7 March 2000 and (b) 24–27 February 2001 (Talley et al., 2003).

6-8
Distress Signals from the Canary in the Coal Mine: Signs of Change in the Global Oceans

Similar events to the 2000–01 incident are marked by the three question marks in figure 6-3. Based on the data, these events seem to have occurred roughly every 20 years.

In other words, current conditions in the Sea of Japan are such that

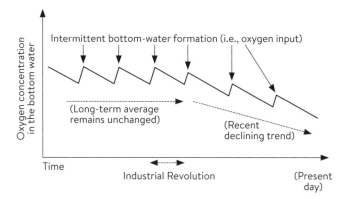

FIGURE 6–8: *Conceptual schematic showing changes in dissolved-oxygen concentration in Japan Sea Bottom Water over time. Spikes in oxygen concentration (indicated by solid arrows) occur only during extremely cold winters, when high-density surface water sinks into the bottom water and temporarily replenishes bottom-water oxygen stores. Although long-term average oxygen concentrations remained almost constant prior to the Industrial Revolution, the long-term average has declined in recent years due to the impacts of global climate change.*

only extremely cold winters, such as the winter of 2000–01, can create surface waters of sufficient density to sink into the bottom water. In the intervals between extremely cold winters, the bottom waters do not receive oxygen input from the surface waters and oxygen concentrations decline. Over time, oxygen concentrations would follow a sawtooth pattern of gradual declines punctuated by occasional downwelling events.

Figure 6-8 shows a schematic representation of this pattern. Prior to the Industrial Revolution, the "peaks" in the sawtooth pattern appear to have happened often enough to maintain bottom-water oxygen concentrations near a constant long-term average.

Although the precise timing of the transition is unknown, in recent years the frequency and volume of bottom-water formation appear to have declined due to the influence of global climate change. The result has been a reduction in the overall rate of oxygen supply into the bottom water, leading to a decline in oxygen concentration. I believe that this change accounts for the 10% decline in oxygen concentration over the past 33 years that I described above.

This decline was only revealed thanks to over three decades of observation dating back to 1977. Now that these data are available, it is critically important that society afford this finding the attention it deserves. If the Sea of Japan is a canary in a coal mine, this oxygen decline is a distress call. We need to recognize the environmental changes that are responsible for this distress.

As if to emphasize the severity of this warning, some recent reports indicate that climate change is also beginning to reduce dissolved-oxygen concentrations in the global oceans. Over several decades, scientists in the Sea of Japan painstakingly built up a cutting-edge, long-term dataset that promises to provide a window into the future of the global oceans. These data should now play a major role in informing our actions going forward.

≈

6-9
What about the Impacts of Ongoing Ocean Acidification?

Higher temperatures and lower oxygen concentrations are not the only challenges facing the Sea of Japan in the future. Here, I will discuss how ocean acidification is also poised to have major environmental impacts.

Seawater is weakly alkaline, and in surface waters, the pH (an indicator of hydrogen ion concentration) is typically about 8.1–8.2 (a pH of 7 indicates a neutral solution). Seawater pH generally decreases with depth, and reaches 7.5–7.8 in the deep-water layer.

Initially, ocean acidification is only expected to impact pH in surface waters. As carbon dioxide concentrations in the atmosphere have increased since the Industrial Revolution, greater amounts of it have dissolved into the surface oceans. This dissolved carbon dioxide reacts with water to form a weak acid known as carbonic acid, which lowers the pH of surface seawater.

The IPCC's Fifth Assessment Report, which I referenced in section 6-1, states that surface-water pH in the global oceans has declined by 0.1 over the last 200 years. In the future, this pH decline will not only continue to progress in the surface-water layer, but will also inevitably spread into the deep ocean.

Ocean acidification is a grave issue that threatens to alter the very chemistry of the oceans. Many marine organisms such as mollusks, corals, and foraminifera depend on the extremely low solubility of calcium carbonate ($CaCO_3$) in seawater to build their shells and skeletons. Yet when seawater becomes more acidic, this solubility increases. This means that calcium carbonate structures become more vulnerable to dissolution. This is an existential threat to organisms that depend on calcium carbonate shells or skeletons. If their survival is imperiled, there are concerns that the effects may ripple across the food web and become an ecosystem-wide crisis.

In reality, ocean acidification is likely to have numerous complex effects on the ocean environment. To give just one example, increased carbon dioxide levels in surface waters may also stimulate photosynthetic activity (see fig. 2-3) in regions with abundant nutrients. In turn, this rise in photosynthesis may boost nutrient cycling between the surface and deep-water layers (see section 4-11). We still have much to learn about how these effects will play out in the future.

≈

6-10
Ocean Acidification Affects the Sea of Japan in a Unique Way

How is ocean acidification affecting the Sea of Japan?

Figure 6-9 shows seawater pH profiles measured in the eastern Japan

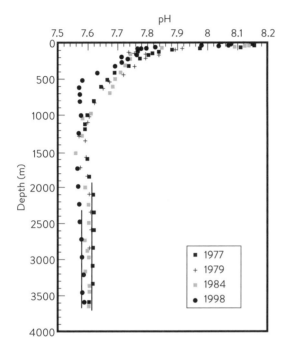

FIGURE 6-9: Changes
in seawater pH in the
eastern Japan Basin.
pH values have been
normalized to 25°C.
Standard pH solutions
obtained from the US
National Bureau of
Standards were used for
calibration.

Basin from 1977 to 1998. Over this 21-year period, surface-water pH declined by 0.06–0.07, indicating that the Sea of Japan is also being affected by the global-scale phenomenon of ocean acidification.

At the same time, however, the figure reveals something unique about the Sea of Japan. Unlike in the global oceans, ocean acidification in the Sea of Japan is already occurring at depth. As can be seen in figure 6-9, pH declines have been observed not just in the deep-water layer, but also in the bottom water, where pH has fallen by about 0.03–0.04 over the same 21-year period.

Surface-water acidification is to be expected, but how could this acidification have already progressed to the bottom water? To my knowledge, the Sea of Japan is the only example anywhere in the world of ocean acidification progressing to such depths so quickly. What does it mean that this phenomenon is occurring in the "miniature ocean" of the Sea of Japan before it takes place in the rest of the world?

The acidification of Japan Sea Bottom Water is related to the decline in bottom-water oxygen concentrations shown in figures 6-2 and 6-3. When organic matter undergoes aerobic decomposition in bottom water, it not only consumes oxygen but also produces carbon dioxide as a byproduct. Because the bottom-water layer is currently largely cut off from the thermohaline circulation, this increases total carbon dioxide (ΣCO_2; see section 3-12) in the bottom water. In turn, this carbon dioxide buildup increases acidity and decreases pH. In other words, the bottom water undergoes acidification.

Scientists are concerned that this same expansion of ocean acidification from the surface to depth will occur in the rest of the world. By paying close attention to the progression of acidification in the Sea of Japan, we can obtain important information about the acidification process itself and help to predict future conditions around the world.

We cannot afford to ignore the warning signals being emitted by the Sea of Japan. In addition to improving the accuracy of pH measurement, we must continue to collect detailed data on pH and other chemical properties (e.g., ΣCO_2 and nutrient levels) to detect new developments in the future.

≋

6-11
Are Japan's Water Resources under Threat?

Recent developments in the progression of global climate change also pose a serious threat to Japan's water cycle. Any weakening of northwesterly monsoon winds could substantially decrease snowfall totals near the Sea of Japan coast. Also, a large enough increase in temperature along the Sea of Japan coast or the mountain ranges that make up the spine of the Japanese archipelago (including the Ou Backbone Range, the Japan Alps, the Chugoku Mountains, and others) would transform much of the precipitation from snow to rain.

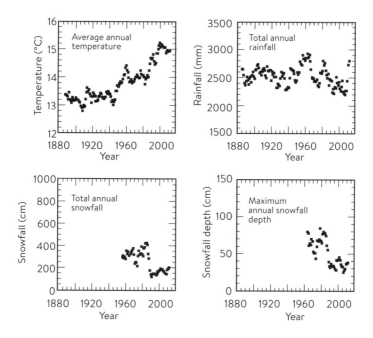

FIGURE 6-10: *Changes in yearly average temperature, total rainfall, total snowfall, and maximum snowfall depth in Kanazawa over the past 130 years. All data points are 5-year moving averages of annual data. Historical weather data were obtained from the Japan Meteorological Agency website.*

You might be thinking that snow and rain are equivalent from the standpoint of water resources. But if you consider what happens after these two forms of precipitation reach the ground, there is a huge difference between them.

As I pointed out in section 1-5-1, snow tends to remain on the ground for some time before melting. When a snowpack melts, it gradually releases meltwater over time. This water can then be absorbed into the soil, and in mountainous regions, is especially likely to be retained in the form of groundwater.

Rain, on the other hand, tends to flow over the soil in the form of runoff. Unless this runoff is captured in a reservoir or other fresh-water body, it will quickly flow through rivers and streams into the sea.

Let us look at the long-term data observed at Kanazawa, which is representative of cities on the Sea of Japan coast (fig. 6-10). Clearly there is an increasing temperature trend, which is likely due to climate change (combined with the urban heat-island effect). At the same time, annual snowfall totals and maximum annual snowfall depths have been declining (unfortunately, the time series for these variables only goes back to around 1960). There does not seem to be a noticeable decline in annual rainfall, however. Taken together, these temporal data indicate that some portion of the precipitation that used to fall as snow is now increasingly falling in the form of rain.

Data for other cities along the Sea of Japan coast such as Wajima and Toyama show similar trends. As mentioned earlier, snow is an extremely important water resource. If snowfall amounts continue to decline, this could portend a worrying future for Japan in which water resources may be insufficient to maintain lush forest ecosystems.

Meteorologist Tetsuzo Yasunari (Director-General of the Research Institute for Humanity and Nature, Japan) addresses the urgency of this issue in a chapter entitled "Chikyu Ondanka to Kan-Nihonkai no Kiko/ Kankyo Henka" (Global Climate Change and Climatic and Environmental Changes in the Sea of Japan Region) in *Nihonkaigaku no Shinseiki* (The New Century of Japan Seaology) vol. 8:

> *The large metropolitan areas along Japan's Pacific coast depend on water and agricultural resources from the Sea of Japan coast, which in turn are maintained by large snowfall totals. In addition to the standard discussions about human causes for global climate change, an equally urgent topic should be ways to evaluate and maintain the systems that human societies currently depend upon for survival but that may be vulnerable to climate shifts and fluctuations (Japan Seaology Promotion Organization, 2008).*

≋

6-12
The Sea of Japan in the Twenty-First Century: Finding Inspiration in the "Upside-Down Map"

Before I close out this chapter, I want to introduce you to a certain map.

This is the *Map of Countries in East Asia and the Sea of Japan Region* (fig. 6-11, plate 5) created by Toyama Prefecture. It's often referred to more simply as the "Upside-Down Map." If you don't recognize the region shown in the map, try rotating the page by 180°, and it will probably become clear to you. This map was first published in 1994, and the version you are seeing now is a revised version issued in 2012. The actual map is available for purchase in color and on B1-sized paper from the website of Toyama Prefecture.

Toyama is home to the headquarters of the United Nations Environment Programme's Northwest Pacific Action Plan, and the prefectural government is actively involved in seeking international cooperation and sustainability around issues concerning the Sea of Japan. As you can probably tell from the Upside-Down Map, the prefecture has a predilection for outside-the-box thinking. Every time I look at this map I can sense my preconceived notions melting away, and I feel as though I can consider the Sea of Japan from a fresh new perspective.

In most maps, the northern margin of the map is placed at the top. This is true of the other maps included in this book. We are so used to this convention that we don't even think about it. In fact, the maps we draw in our heads of places like the Sea of Japan or the Japanese archipelago are invariably oriented with north at the top of the map. I fear that this is evidence of how our modes of thinking have become standardized and constrained. Of course, this standardization is useful in maps with practical applications such as weather forecasting and navigation, but I believe that maps can also play a different role. Sometimes, maps can be a fun way to stimulate thoughts and let new ideas fly.

The Upside-Down Map feels new and fresh compared to maps that are oriented in the standard direction, and it helps me to consider the geography of the Sea of Japan—the pattern of land and sea—in

FIGURE 6-11: Map of countries in East Asia and the Sea of Japan region. Reproduced with permission from Toyama Prefecture.

unfamiliar ways. For example, one thing I noticed while looking at this map is the beautiful arrangement of the various archipelagos (the Aleutian Islands, the Japanese archipelago, and the Nansei Islands) with their backbone mountain ranges drawing graceful arcs between the Eurasian continent and the Pacific Ocean.

When humans first reached the eastern margin of the Eurasian continent some 30,000–40,000 years ago, they would have looked upon the sea that stretched out before them (the Sea of Japan) in amazement. It seems natural to think that the maps they drew in their heads in this moment placed the continent beneath their feet at the bottom margin and the ocean they were about to cross at the top. This mirrors the arrangement of the Upside-Down Map itself.

In his book *The Clash of Civilizations and the Remaking of World Order*, the American political scientist Samuel P. Huntington groups the cultures of the world into seven or eight "major civilizations."

Under this categorization scheme, Japan is classified on its own as one of the major civilizations because of the ways in which it differs from all other cultures. For example, the Japanese civilization is considered clearly distinct from the Sinic (Chinese-influenced) civilization, which is another of the major civilizations. The foundations of Japanese civilization were nurtured under the geographic and climatic conditions of the Jomon period and subsequent eras. As I have already explained in previous sections, the Sea of Japan played a vital role throughout this history as a buffer zone between the Eurasian continent and the Japanese archipelago.

I believe that the best aspects of Japanese culture and its value systems (e.g., respect for the natural world, compassion for the disadvantaged, integrity, and inherent aversion to unfairness) came about as a result of interactions with the Sea of Japan region, which was considered Japan's "front door" for much of its history. By living in harmony with the Sea of Japan, the people of the Japanese archipelago learned to coexist with nature, to love the land on which they lived, and to adopt a sustainable lifestyle.

In this book, I have discussed various aspects of the Sea of Japan including its deep-water circulation and climate systems. In addition, I have explained how the people of the Sea of Japan region benefited from these systems, interacted with each other, and created the Sea of Japan Cultural Region. You have now learned that although the Sea of Japan may be a very small sea (it truly warrants the nickname "miniature ocean"), the benefits it provides are of critical importance to the Japanese archipelago.

I can't help but think that the Sea of Japan, which has been such a constant presence throughout Japanese history, also holds the key to restoring the best aspects of Japanese culture and many lessons for our modern society. I am convinced that a renewed awareness of the benefits and importance of the Sea of Japan will spur new ideas and developments for the future.

At this moment in the twenty-first century, all of humanity must address a host of serious challenges around the world including dealing with the impacts of anthropogenic climate change and finding a sustainable model for global environmental conservation. The Upside-Down Map of the Sea of Japan may offer useful inspiration for finding these urgently-needed answers.

~~~~~~~~~~~~~~~~~~~~~~~~~~~~ *Column 6* ~~~~~~~~~~~~~~~~~~~~~~~~~~~~

Oceanographic Cruises aboard the *Hakuho Maru*

I have mentioned the oceanographic research vessel *Hakuho Maru* in numerous sections of this book. In fact, I myself have participated in many research cruises aboard this ship.

What is an oceanographic research cruise like? To illustrate a typical cruise aboard the *Hakuho Maru*, I will now provide a timeline of the cruise KH-10-2 (Chief Scientist: Professor Jing Zhang of the University of Toyama), which was conducted in the Sea of Japan and the western North Pacific in June–July 2010.

The *Hakuho Maru* departed Tokyo Port on 11 June with a full complement of 35 researchers together with 36 crew and headed north along the east coast of Honshu before entering the Sea of Japan through the Tsugaru Strait. The ship stopped at 18 sampling sites, where researchers took seawater samples (see fig. 6-12) and conducted other observations, before heading into port at Hakodate on 19 June. Here, some of the researchers disembarked and others arrived on board.

On 21 June, the ship departed Hakodate with 34 researchers and the same crew. After stopping at 13 sampling sites located offshore of the east coast of Hokkaido in the western North Pacific and Sea of Okhotsk, the ship returned to the Sea of Japan via the La Pérouse Strait and continued observations at 31 additional sites.

On 14 July, the ship docked at Hakata Port (on the island of Kyushu), where additional researchers disembarked and others arrived on board. The ship departed Hakata Port on 17 July with 23 researchers and the crew, stopped at 13 sampling sites in the Sea of Japan, and then traveled through the Tsugaru Strait to the Sanriku region before arriving at the Port of Yokohama on 23 July. This marked the end of a successful research cruise.

Similar research cruises can take as little as 20 days or last as long as 3

~~~~~~

~~~~~~~~~~~~~~~~~~~~~~~ *Column 6* ~~~~~~~~~~~~~~~~~~~~~~~

months according to the planned study sites and purposes. Researchers from various academic fields participate in these cruises, which typically occur about 5–10 times a year.

The *Hakuho Maru* is currently operated by the Japan Agency for Marine-Earth Science and Technology (JAMSTEC), which manages all of the hardware needed for each voyage. JAMSTEC's responsibilities include maintaining the ship and its on-board equipment, deciding on the number of ship days and loading fuel accordingly, procuring the crew (other than the captain), sailing the ship to the study area, and conducting observations.

Although maintaining a ship to operate research cruises is enormously costly, these costs are paid for by government grants. Usually, none of the money needed to operate the ship comes from the researchers that participate in the cruises.

The content of the scientific research conducted aboard the *Hakuho Maru*, or in other words, the agenda of each research cruise, is determined through a bottom-up selection process that involves the researchers submitting individual research proposals. Marine researchers from universities and research institutions all over Japan submit research proposals for this purpose. These proposals are evaluated, and final selections are made by the Cooperative Research Vessel Steering Committee (hereinafter referred to as "the Committee") located at the Atmosphere and Ocean Research Institute at the University of Tokyo. Eighteen marine researchers representing universities and research institutions across the country serve three-year terms on the Committee.

Researchers hoping to initiate a cruise on the *Hakuho Maru* must submit a proposal to the Committee that details their intended research purpose and methods, specific plans for ship time, list of prospective

~~~~~~~~~~~~~~~~~~~~~~~~ *Column 6* ~~~~~~~~~~~~~~~~~~~~~~~~

passengers, observation equipment required, past scientific achieve-ments, etc. This process tests the limits of many researcher's proposal-writing abilities. In addition, the researchers must also explain the impor-tance and novelty of their proposed research in an easy-to-understand manner at a public symposium hosted by the Committee, and must give satisfactory answers to any questions posed to them. The Committee will then compile the results of their evaluation and assign a score to each proposal. Proposals that earn the most points get first priority when deciding on cruise schedules.

Because this process is carried out only once every three years, the *Hakuho Maru*'s activities are generally planned out three years at a time. Drawing up plans for such a long span of time at once allows the Com-mittee to be as flexible as possible when combining the various research projects (which might each entail different study sites, seasons, and lengths of observation) into as few ship days as possible. Also, this allows ample time for preparation. For example, if a cruise is scheduled to enter another country's EEZ, an application must be submitted to that country at least six months in advance.

Some time, however, is set aside for last-minute additions. Some por-tion of the annual ship days (about 30 days in total) are reserved for time-sensitive research projects, and proposals to fill these days are accepted a year in advance. Of course, it goes without saying that these additional proposals must also pass a strict review process.

Operation of the *Hakuho Maru* was transferred from the University of Tokyo to JAMSTEC in April 2004. Immediately after this transfer, the number of annual ship days increased by some 60% to 285 days, which was a great boon to marine scientists nationwide. Unfortunately, this number has declined in subsequent years. As of 2015, partly due to

~~~~~~

~~~~~~~~~~~~~~~~~~~~~~~~~~~ **Column 6** ~~~~~~~~~~~~~~~~~~~~~~~~~~~

FIGURE 6-12: Taking water samples using a bundle of Niskin bottles during cruise KH-10-2.

budget cuts and rising oil prices, the number of ship days had fallen back to pre-transfer levels.

The *Hakuho Maru* is an oceanographic research vessel with a bottom-up selection process that provides an important platform for basic research and graduate student education—two fundamental building blocks of Japanese academics. The decline in ship days is a major source of concern for those hoping that these building blocks will continue to be maintained and further developed in the future.

Epilogue

In this book, I have touched upon the vital importance of the "Mother Sea" (the Sea of Japan) to the Japanese archipelago from a variety of perspectives.

Geographically, the Sea of Japan and the Japanese archipelago exist cheek-to-jowl. Every day, residents of the Japanese archipelago receive countless benefits from the Sea of Japan. Despite this, many Japanese people do not fully appreciate the Sea of Japan's importance. There are many possible reasons for this. Compared to Japan's bright and spacious Pacific coast, its Sea of Japan coast is often considered dreary and dull. Perhaps, among Japanese people, there is also a subconscious urge to ignore the Sea of Japan to avoid contemplating the difficult history we share with countries on its opposite shore.

Regardless, it strikes me as unnatural and improvident for Japanese people to not express interest in or appreciate the value of this sea in our own backyard. If Japan is to play a leading role in developing a sustainable society for the future, I believe its citizens must acquire a proper understanding and appreciation of how the warm and humid climate of the Japanese archipelago and other benefits provided by the Sea of Japan enabled the development of Japanese civilization beginning in the Jomon period.

Of course, there is little danger that the Sea of Japan itself will disappear in the future. However, there is a real risk that ongoing human activities will continue to gradually alter its oceanography, including its chemical properties and climate. Furthermore, change in the Sea of Japan will profoundly affect the Japanese archipelago. We are responsible for conserving the environment of the Sea of Japan and passing it on to the next generation.

In section 4-3, I wrote about the exquisite timing of the geological events that resulted in the Sea of Japan reaching its optimal size just as the first humans arrived in the Japanese archipelago. In truth, I am not the only person to have made this observation. Many earlier writers have noted this same accident of timing. Although I was not conscious of this initially, while reading over the first draft of this book and reviewing the relevant literature, I was reminded of many of such instances.

For example, the following passage appears in the seismologist and geophysicist Hideki Shimamura's *Nihonkai no Mokushiroku* (Revelations of the Sea of Japan, 1994):

> *Although the Sea of Japan has a pervasive influence on the nation of Japan today, throughout much of Earth's history, the Sea of Japan did not even exist. In other words, from a geological perspective, the Sea of Japan is quite young.*
>
> *The deep connections between the Sea of Japan and the nation of Japan cannot be understood without first considering why the Sea of Japan came to exist, and why it reached its current size.*
>
> *If the Sea of Japan were 10 times larger than it is today, that is, if Japan were located 10 times farther away from the Eurasian continent, the Japanese archipelago would be a remote island chain with a vastly different history.*
>
> *Conversely, if the Sea of Japan didn't exist, or if it existed but were 10 times smaller than it is today, this would also have radically altered the course of Japanese history. In this scenario, the Japanese archipelago would have remained either part of or extremely close to the Eurasian continent, and the nation of Japan might never have emerged at all.*

Similarly, the world-renowned aurora expert Shun'ichi Akasofu makes the following claim in his essay "Nihonkai kara Omou Koto" (Thoughts Stemming from the Sea of Japan), which appeared in *Nihonkaigaku no Shinseiki* (The New Century of Japan Seaology) edited by the Japan Seaology Promotion Conference (2001):

> *How important is the Sea of Japan to the nation of Japan? From a historical perspective, without the barrier that the Sea of Japan provides against*

invasion from the continent, it is possible that the nation of Japan would not exist today. Or if Japan did exist, its history would be unimaginably different. Similarly, from an earth science perspective, I suspect that the benefits provided by the Sea of Japan are too vast to imagine. It would be interesting to run a computer simulation of a scenario in which the Sea of Japan didn't exist: that is, in which the Sea of Japan was replaced by dry land. Such a simulation would reveal many of the benefits that the Sea of Japan provides. Although this is just speculation, I suspect that the simulation would show that if the Sea of Japan were dry land, it would become a desert. In winter, an Arctic air mass with temperatures around −50°C would roll across this desert and reach the shores of the Japanese archipelago. This is what the Sea of Japan protects us from: cold continental air masses. Specifically, when continental air masses cross the Sea of Japan, they come into contact with the warm sea surface and absorb water vapor. This vapor is then carried to the Sea of Japan coast and the Ou Backbone Range, where it falls as rain or snow. Without this input of water vapor, places such as Akita, Niigata, and Toyama would most likely be unsuitable for rice production.

Finally, the following passage is contained in the journalist Yoshiko Sakurai's *Nihonjin no Bitoku* (Japanese Virtues; Sakurai 2008):

> *Sometimes, when I see Japan on a world map, I think the sun is to the Earth as the Earth is to Japan.*
>
> *What I mean is that the Earth owes many of its current characteristics to its position relative to the sun. It is not so close to the sun as to be burned by the sun's rays, and not so far away as to be left in the cold. Moreover, thanks to its distance from Jupiter and Saturn, it is protected from meteorite impacts that could endanger the global environment. On Earth, Japan is neither too close nor too far from the Eurasian continent and is surrounded on all sides by a rich marine environment. This is why I believe that Japan has truly been blessed by geography.*

Even in my limited reading, I came across all of these writers who have noticed and underlined the importance of the Sea of Japan. I have no doubt that there are countless others I am not aware of who have made similar assertions. It is encouraging to know that my ideas are shared by so many.

While working on this book, I was greatly helped in two ways by the UTokyo Ocean Alliance:

First, in collaboration with the Nippon Foundation and the Northwest Pacific Region Environmental Cooperation Center (NPEC), the Ocean Alliance organized two large symposia about the Sea of Japan for the general public.

The first symposium, entitled *Nihonkai: Chiisana Umi no Okina Megumi* (The Sea of Japan: Big Benefits from a Small Sea), was held in Tokyo at the Nihonbashi Mitsukoshi department store, main branch, on 10–16 July 2013. This free event centered around academic lectures and panel discussions but also included poster sessions and an exhibition of products created in the Sea of Japan region. I was involved in coordinating the whole event and undertook the preparations and implementation with the help of my colleagues Dr. Shingo Kimura and Dr. Mitsuo Yamamoto. I also hosted one of the lectures, entitled *Moshimo Nihonkai ga Sonzai Shinakattara* (What If the Sea of Japan Didn't Exist?) where I introduced a general audience to some of the more fascinating aspects of the Sea of Japan.

Subsequently, on 1 March 2014, with the help of NPEC's Takafumi Yoshida, a second symposium entitled *Nihonkai: Himerareta Kanosei* (The Sea of Japan: Hidden Possibilities) was held in Toyama City on the Sea of Japan coast.

Each of these symposia was attended by several hundred people, and I was reminded once again of just how many people want to learn more about the Sea of Japan. I felt strongly that instead of letting the excitement of these events fade away, it was important to put at least some of the information that had been presented about the Sea of Japan into writing. This became my immediate motivation for writing this book. As such, the conversations and questions and answers from the lectures and panel discussions contributed to many passages in this book. I am profoundly grateful to everyone who attended the events and participated in the discussions.

The second way in which I was helped by the UTokyo Ocean Alliance was through their "visiting lectures" program. As part of its outreach activities, the Ocean Alliance arranges for professors to teach classes around the country in response to requests from elementary, middle, and high schools. I am occasionally asked to participate in this program, and in 2015, I received two separate requests to teach middle schoolers about the Sea of Japan.

I taught the first class on 14 July at Noto Choritsu Ogi Junior High School in Ishikawa Prefecture, within sight of the Sea of Japan itself. I taught the second class, on 28 November, at Yokoyama Junior High School in Hachioji City, Tokyo. The class at Ogi Junior High School was called *Kyoi no Nihonkai: Sono Kako to Genzai* (The Incredible Sea of Japan: Its Past and Present), and the one at Yokoyama Junior High School was called *Nihonkai to wa Donna Umi Daro?* (What Is the Sea of Japan Like?). Each class lasted around an hour.

Before this, I had never talked to middle schoolers about the Sea of Japan. I thought long and hard about how to convey the splendor and importance of the Sea of Japan in an accessible way, and ended up using many of the figures that appear in this book. The students at Ogi Junior High School (46 students) and the eighth-graders at Yokoyama Junior High School (167 students) were all attentive throughout and asked many excellent questions. These classes were truly wonderful experiences.

I believe that the sense of accomplishment I got from teaching these classes gave me the energy I needed to finish this book. I am indebted not just to the students but also to the teachers and school-board members who assisted me at each school.

While writing this book, I gleaned many useful details from books and articles. Although I have listed as many of these as possible in the bibliography at the end of the book, the sheer number of review articles and the like meant that not all of them could be included. Please forgive me for these omissions.

Both Mr. Takashi Kurata at the Kodansha Bluebacks Editorial Department and Dr. Naoki Hosaka, senior researcher at the UTokyo Ocean Alliance, provided invaluable advice during and after the planning stage of this book. Mr. Kurata also provided numerous edits and suggestions to the rough drafts. Dr. Kyoko Okino at the Atmosphere and Ocean Research Institute, the University of Tokyo, kindly made a detailed bathymetric map of the Sea of Japan. For their help, I offer my deepest thanks.

February 2016
Toshitaka Gamo

BIBLIOGRAPHY
Journal articles, reviews, and chapters (in alphabetical order by author)

Bintanja, R. et al. 2005. "Modeled Atmospheric Temperatures and Global Sea Levels over the Past Million Years." *Nature* 437: 125–128.

Danchenkov, M.A. et al. 2006. "A History of Physical Oceanographic Research in the Japan/East Sea." *Oceanography* 19(3): 18–31.

Eddy, J.A. 1981. "Climate and the Role of the Sun." In *Climate and History*, edited by Rotberg, R.I. and T.K. Rabb, 145–167. Princeton University Press.

Gamo, T. and Y. Horibe. 1983. "Abyssal Circulation in the Japan Sea." *Journal of the Oceanographical Society of Japan* 39: 220–230.

Gamo, T. et al. 1986. "Spacial and Temporal Variations of Water Characteristics in the Japan Sea Bottom Layer." *Journal of Marine Research* 44: 781–793.

Gamo, T. 1995. "Nihonkai no Teisojunkan" [Bottom Circulation in the Sea of Japan]. *Kagaku* [Science] 65: 316–323.

Gamo, T. 1999. "Global Warming May Have Slowed Down the Deep Conveyor Belt of a Marginal Sea of the Northwestern Pacific: Japan Sea." *Geophysical Research Letters* 26: 3137–3140.

Gamo, T. et al. 2001. "Recent Upward Shift of the Deep Convection System in the Japan Sea, as Inferred from the Geochemical Tracers Tritium, Oxygen, and Nutrients." *Geophysical Research Letters* 28: 4143–4146.

Gamo, T. 2011. "Dissolved Oxygen in the Bottom Water of the Sea of Japan as a Sensitive Alarm for Global Climate Change." *Trends in Analytical Chemistry* 30: 1308–1319.

Gamo, T. 2013. "Izumo Bunka o Hagukunda Nihonkai wa Donoyona Umika" [The Sea of Japan: What Is It like and How Did It Nurture Izumo Culture?]. *Gendai Shisou* [Modern Thought] 41(December Special Issue), Special Feature on Izumo. Edited by S. Miura, 216–221.

Gamo, T. et al. 2014. "The Sea of Japan and Its Unique Chemistry Revealed by Time-Series Observations over the Last 30 Years." *Monographs on Environment, Earth and Planets* 2(1): 1–22.

Kim, K-R. et al. 2002. "A Sudden Bottom-Water Formation during the Severe Winter 2000–2001: The Case of the East/Japan Sea." *Geophysical Research Letters* 29(8): 75-1-75-4. doi: 10.1029/2001GL014498.

Koizumi, I. 1995. "Nihonkinkai no Kairyukei wa Myakudoshiteita" [Ocean Currents near Japan are Fluctuating]. In *Koza: Bunmei to Kankyo Daiikkan "Chikyu to Bunmei no Shuki"* [Lecture: Civilization and the Environment Vol. 1—Periodicity in Civilizations and the Environment], edited by Koizumi, I. and Y. Yasuda, 62–77. Asakura Shoten.

Kudo, T. and M. Ogasawara. 2009. "Chishitsu Johoten 2008 Akita / Akita no Chishitsu 'Akita no Daichi o Katachizukuru mono' [Geological Information Exhibition 2008 Akita / The Geology of Akita 'What Shapes Akita's Landscape?']". *Chishisu Nyuusu* [Geological News] 658: 18–20.

Kumamoto, Y. et al. 2008. "Temporal and Spatial Variations of Radiocarbon in Japan Sea Bottom

Water." *Journal of Oceanography* 64: 429–441.

Matsui, H., R. Tada, and T. Oba. 1998. "Saishuhyoki no Kaisuijunhendo ni taisuru Nihonkai no Oto" [Response of the Sea of Japan to Sea Level Changes during the Last Glacial Period]. *Daiyonki Kenkyu* [Quaternary Studies] 37: 221–233.

Minami, H., Y. Kano, and K. Ogawa. 1999. "Long-term Variations of Potential Temperature and Dissolved Oxygen of the Japan Sea Proper Water." *Journal of Oceanography* 55: 197–205.

Mori, K. 1993. "Kodai Nihonkaibunka to Sekiko" [Lagoons, Harbors, and the Ancient Cultures of the Sea of Japan]. In *Umi, Kata, Nihonjin: Nihonkaibunmei Koryuken* [Oceans, Lagoons, and the Japanese People: Cultural Exchange in the Sea of Japan Cultural Region], edited by Umehara, T. and S. Ito, 9–35. Kodansha.

Nitani, H. 1972. "On the Deep and Bottom Waters in the Japan Sea." In *Researches in Hydrography and Oceanography*, edited by Shoji, D., 151–201. Hydrographic Department.

Oba, T. 1983. "Saishuhyokiiko no Nihonkai no Kokankyo." [Paleoenvironment of the Sea of Japan since the Last Glacial Period]. *Gekkan Chikyu* [Earth Monthly] 5: 37–46.

Oba, T. et al. 1991. "Paleoenvironmental Changes in the Japan Sea during the Last 85,000 Years." *Paleoceanography* 6: 499–518.

Senju, T. et al. 2002. "Renewal of the Bottom Water after the Winter 2000-2001 May Spin-up the Thermohaline Circulation in the Japan Sea." *Geophysical Research Letters* 29(7): 53-1–53-3. doi: 10.1029/2001GL014093.

Senju, T. et al. 2005. "Deep Flow Field in the Japan/East Sea as Deduced from Direct Current Measurements." *Deep-Sea Research* II 52: 1726–1741.

Stuiver, M., P.D. Quay, and H.G. Ostlund. 1983. "Abyssal Water Carbon-14 Distribution and the Age of the World Oceans." *Science* 219: 849–851.

Suda, K. 1932. "Nihonkai no Teisosui ni Tsuite (Yoho)" [On the Bottom Waters of the Sea of Japan (Forecast)]. *Kaiyo Jiho*: 4(1): 221–240.

Tada, R. 1995. "Nihon to Ajiya o Musubu Saishuhyoki no Rikkyo" [A Land Bridge Existed between Japan and the Eurasian Continent during the Last Glacial Period]. In *Koza: Bunmei to Kankyo Daijukkan "Umi to Bunmei"* [Lecture: Civilization and the Environment Vol. 10—Civilization and the Oceans], edited by Koizumi I. and K. Tanaka, 31–48. Asakura Shoten.

Tada, R. 1997. "Saishuhyokiiko no Nihonkai oyobi Shuheniki no Kankyohensen" [Environmental Changes in and around the Sea of Japan since the Last Glacial Period]. *Daiyonki Kenkyu* [Quaternary Studies] 36(5): 287–300.

Talley, L.D. et al. 2003. "Deep Convection and Brine Rejection in the Japan Sea." *Geophysical Research Letters* 30(4): 8-1–8-4. doi: 10.1029/2002GL016451.

Talley, L.D. et al. 2006. "Japan/East Sea Water Masses and Their Relation to the Sea's Circulation." *Oceanography* 19(3): 32–49.

Tsunogai, S. 1981. "Taiheiyo oyobi Taiseiyo Shinsosui no Nenreiketteiho to Sono Oyo" [A Method for Determining the Age of Pacific and Atlantic Deep Water and Its Application]. *Chikyu Kagaku* [Geochemistry] 15: 70–76.

Uda, M. 1934. "Nihonkai oyobi Sono Rinsetsukaiku no Kaikyo" [Oceanography of the Sea of Japan and Its Nearby Waters]. *Suisan Shikenjo Hokoku* [Journal of the Imperial Fisheries Experimental Station] 5: 57–190.

Zhang, J. and H. Satake. 2003. "The Chemical Characteristics of Submarine Groundwater Seepage in Toyama Bay, Central Japan." In *Land and Marine Hydrogeology*, edited by Taniguchi, M. et al., 45–60. Elsevier.

English books (in alphabetical order by author)
Broecker, W.S. 2010. *The Great Ocean Conveyor: Discovering the Trigger for Abrupt Climate Change.* Princeton University Press.

Broecker, W.S. and T-H. Peng. 1982. *Tracers in the Sea.* Eldigio Press.

Defant, A. 1961. *Physical Oceanography (vol. I).* Pergamon Press.

Horibe, Y. 1981. *Preliminary Report of the Hakuhō Maru Cruise KH-77-3 (Pegasus Expedition).* Ocean Research Institute, University of Tokyo.

IPCC. 2013. Summary for Policymakers. In: *Climate Change 2013: The Physical Science Basis. Contribution of Working Group I to the Fifth Assessment Report of the Intergovernmental Panel on Climate Change.* Edited by Stocker, T.F., D. Qin, G.-K. Plattner, M. Tignor, S.K. Allen, J. Boschung, A. Nauels, Y. Xia, V. Bex and P.M. Midgley. Cambridge University Press.

Japan Meteorological Agency. 1971. *The Results of Marine Meteorological and Oceanographical Observations.* no. 46.

The Oceanography Society. 2006. *Special Issue on the Japan/East Sea. Oceanography* 19(3).

Japanese books (in alphabetical order by author)
Adachi, H. 1998. *Nihon no Fune: Wasenhen* [Japanese Ships: Wasen Edition]. *Nippon Kaiji Kagaku Shinko Zaidan Fune no Kagakukan* [Japan Maritime Science Foundation Museum of Maritime Science].

Atmosphere and Ocean Research Institute, The University of Tokyo 50th Anniversary Project Preparation Committee (ed.) 2013. *Tokyo Daigaku Taiki Kaiyo Kenkyusho Gojunenshi 1962–2012* [Fifty Years of the Atmosphere and Ocean Research Institute, The University of Tokyo: 1962–2012]. Atmosphere and Ocean Research Institute, The University of Tokyo.

Fujioka, K. and D. Hirata, eds. 2014. *Nihonkai no Kakudai to Izuko no Shototsu* [Expansion of the Sea of Japan and Collision of the Izu Arc]. Yurindo.

Fujita, F. 1990. *Kodai no Nihonkai Bunka* [Ancient Cultures of the Sea of Japan]. Chuokoron Shinsha.

Gamo, T., ed. 2014. *Kaiyo Chikyukagaku* [Marine Geochemistry]. Kodansha.

Gamo, T. and A. Takeuchi, eds. 2006. *Umi no Chikara (Nihonkaigaku no Shinseiki 6)* [The New Century of Japan Seaology 6: The Power of the Ocean]. Kadokawa Shoten.

Hidaka, K. 1968. *Kaiyogaku tono Yonjunen* [Forty Years with Oceanography]. NHK Publishing.

Huntington, S.P. 2000. *Bunmei no Shototsu to 21 Seiki no Nihon* [The Clash of Civilizations and Japan in the 21st Century]. Translated by C. Suzuki, Shueisha.

Intoh, M., ed. 2012. *Jinrui Daiido: Afurika kara Isutato e* [Human Migration: From Africa to Easter Island]. Asahi Shimbun Publications.

Ishii, K. 1995a. *Mono to Ningen no Bunkashi 76-I Wasen I* [Cultural History of People and Objects 76-I: Wasen I]. Hosei University Press.

Ishii, K. 1995b. *Mono to Ningen no Bunkashi 76-II Wasen II* [Cultural History of People and Objects 76-II: Wasen II]. Hosei University Press.

Ishii, K., ed. 2002. *Nihon no Fune o Fukugen Suru: Kodai kara Kinsei Made* [Restoring Japanese Ships: From Ancient to Early Modern]. Gakken.

Japan Seaology Promotion Conference, ed. 2001. *Nihonkaigaku no Shinseiki* [The New Century of Japanese Seaology]. Kadokawa Shoten.

Japan Seaology Promotion Organization, ed. 2008. *Nihonkai: Kako kara Mirai e (Nihonkaigaku no Shinseiki 8 Soshuhen)* [The New Century of Japan Seaology 8 (Compendium): The Sea of Japan: Its Past and Future]. Kadokawa Gakugei Publishing.

Kato, I. et al. 1972. *Umi (Tokyo Daigaku Kokai Koza 15)* [University of Tokyo Open Lecture 15: The Ocean]. University of Tokyo Press.

Kitahara, T. 1921. *Kaiyo Kenkyu: Gyoson Yawa* [Ocean Research: Evening Lectures for Fishing Villages]. Japan Fisheries Association.

Kobayashi, M. 2006. *Kodai Nihonkaibunmei Koryuken: Yurashia no Bunmeihendo no Naka de* [The Ancient Sea of Japan Cultural Exchange Region: In the Midst of Eurasian Civilizational Change]. Sekaishisosha.

Koizumi, I., ed. 2003. *Junkan Suru Umi to Mori (Nihonkaigaku no Shinseiki 3)* [The New Century of Japan Seaology 3: Forest and Ocean Cycling]. Kadokawa Shoten.

Koizumi, I. 2006. *Nihonkai to Kannihonkai Chiiki: Sono Seiritsu to Shizenkankyo no Hensen* [The Sea of Japan and Sea of Japan Region: Its Formation and Environmental Fluctuations]. Kadokawa Gakugei Shuppan.

La Pérouse, J-F.d.G. 1988. *Raperuzu Sekai Shukoki Nihonkinkai Hen* [The Voyage of La Pérouse around the World: Japan and Nearby Seas]. Translated by T. Kobayashi. Hakusuisha.

Makino, R. 1979. *Kitamaebune no Jidai: Kinsei Igono Nihonkai Kaiunshi* [The Age of Kitamae Ships: A History of Shipping in Japan since the Early Modern Age]. Kyoikusha.

Matsumoto, R., Y. Okuda, and Y. Aoki. 1994. *Metan Haidoreto* [Methane Hydrates]. Nikkei Science.

Mizoguchi, Y. 2011. *Afurika de Tanjo shita Jinrui ga Nihonjin ni Narumade* [From the Rise of Humans in Africa to the Emergence of Japanese People]. SB Creative.

Mori, K., ed. 1983. *Shinpojiumu: Kodai Nihonkai Bunka* [Symposium: Ancient Cultures of the Sea of Japan]. Shogakukan.

Nakano, M. 2015. *Nihonkai Monogatari: Sekaichizu kara no Tabi* [The Sea of Japan Story: Journey from a World Map]. Iwanami Shoten.

National Astronomical Observatory of Japan. 2019. Chronological Scientific Tables. Maruzen.

NHK Special Japanese Project, ed. 2001. *Nihonjin Harukana Tabi Daisankan: Umi ga Sodateta Mori no Okoku* [Faraway Japanese Travels Vol. 3: A Forest Kingdom Nurtured by the Sea]. NHK Publishing.

Noda, S. 2008. *Nihonkai wa Dodekitaka (Sosho Chikyu Hakken 12)* [Earth Discovery Series 12: How the Sea of Japan Was Born]. Nakanishiya Publishing.

Sakurai, Y. 2008. *Nihonjin no Bitoku: Hokoriaru Nihonjin ni Naro* [Japanese Virtues: Becoming a Proud Japanese Person]. Takarajimasha.

Shimamura, H. 1994. *Nihonkai no Mokushiroku* [Revelations of the Sea of Japan]. Sangokan.

Suda, K. 1933. *Kaiyo Kagaku* [Marine Science]. Kokon Shoin.

Taira, A. 1990. *Nihonretto no Tanjo* [The Birth of the Japanese Archipelago]. Iwanami Shoten.

Takase, S. 1984. *Nihonkai Bunka no Keisei* [Development of Sea of Japan Cultures]. Meicho Shuppan.

Tanabe, H. et al. 2010. *Chimei no Hassei to Kino: Nihonkai Chimei no Kenkyu* [Origin and Function of Geographic Names: Study of Geographic Names in the Sea of Japan]. Teikyo University Geographic Name Study Group.

Tanii, K. 2015. *Fune o Kaibo Suru: Tanii Kenzo Genga no Sekai* [Analyzing Ships: The World of Kenzo Tanii's Paintings]. NYK Maritime Museum Exhibition Catalog.

Tanii, K. and N. Tanii. 2010. *Nihon no Fune: Umi kara Mita Nihonshi* [Japanese Ships: Japanese History from a Marine Perspective]. Uozu High School Eighth Reunion Committee (Class of 1956).

Tsutsumi, Y. 2014. *E de Wakaru Nihonretto no Tanjo* [The Emergence of the Japanese Archipelago in Pictures]. Kodansha.

Uda, M. 1941. *Umi no Tankyushi* [A History of Ocean Exploration]. Kawade Shobo Shinsha.

Uda, M. 1971. *Umi ni Ikite: Kaiyo Kenkyusha no Kaiso* [A Life of the Sea: Recollections of an Oceanographer]. Tokai University Press.

Uda, M. 1978. *Kaiyo Kenkyu Hattatsushi (Kaiyo Kagaku Kiso Koza Hokan)* [History of Research and Development in Marine Science: Supplement to an Introductory Course in Marine Science]. Tokai University Press.

Umehara, T. and S. Ito, eds. 1993. *Umi, Kata, Nihonjin: Nihonkaibunmei Koryuken* [Oceans, Lagoons, and the Japanese People: Cultural Exchange in the Sea of Japan Cultural Region]. Kodansha.

Yamada, Y. 2012. *Odoroita! Shiranakatta Nihonkokkyo no Shinjijitsu* [Amazing! New Facts You Didn't Know about the Japanese Border]. Jitsugyo no Nihon Sha.

Yomiuri Shimbun Hokuriku Branch, ed. 2015. *Hokuriku kara Mita Nihonshi* [Japanese History from the Perspective of the Hokuriku Region]. Yosensha.

ABOUT THE AUTHOR

Toshitaka Gamo is professor emeritus at the University of Tokyo. Born in Nagano Prefecture in 1952, he received his BS and PhD from the Department of Chemistry at the University of Tokyo School of Science and specializes in chemical oceanography. Previously, he was a professor at the Hokkaido University Graduate School of Science, and at the Ocean Research Institute and the Atmosphere and Ocean Research Institute, both at the University of Tokyo. Prof. Gamo has dedicated his career to developing and using new observation technologies for chemical oceanography. Thanks to his passion for fieldwork using ships and submersibles, he has accumulated some 1740 ship days and participated in 15 deep-sea submersible dives over the course of his career. He has published numerous studies on deep ocean circulation and seafloor hydrothermal activity, and has been the recipient of various awards, including the Oceanographic Society of Japan Prize, the Geochemistry Research Association Science Prize (also known as the Miyake Prize), and the Prime Minister's Commendations for Contributors to Promote the Country as a Maritime Nation. His distinguished lecture on his research on the Sea of Japan won high acclaim at the 2013 Asia Oceania Geosciences Society Annual Meeting (held in Brisbane, Australia). His other books include *Kaiyo no Kagaku* (Ocean Science; NHK Publishing, Inc.), *Kaiyo Chikyu Kagaku* (Marine Geochemistry; Kodansha), and *Taiheiyo: Sono Shinso de Okotteiru Koto* (The Pacific Ocean: What is Happening in the Deep?; Kodansha).

ABOUT THE TRANSLATOR

Gen Del Raye: A native speaker of Japanese and English, Gen Del Raye was born and raised in Kyoto, Japan and earned a BS and MS in biology from Stanford University and a PhD in oceanography from the University of Hawai'i at Mānoa. His translations of scientific manuscripts have been published in *Advances in Remote Sensing* and *Limnology and Oceanography: Methods*, among others. Dr. Del Raye currently lives in Minneapolis, Minnesota.

（英文版）日本海：その深層で起こっていること
The Sea of Japan: Unraveling the Mystery of Its Hidden Depths

2021 年 3 月 27 日　第 1 刷発行

著　者　　蒲生俊敬
訳　者　　デルレイ 弦
発行所　　一般財団法人出版文化産業振興財団
　　　　　〒 101-0051 東京都千代田区神田神保町 2-2-30
　　　　　電話　03-5211-7283
　　　　　ホームページ　https://www.jpic.or.jp/

印刷・製本所　大日本印刷株式会社

© 2016 Toshitaka Gamo
Printed in Japan
ISBN 978-4-86658-129-3